Powerful Prayers and Psalm 23

The Practical Mystic's guide to three Christian prayers: The Lord is my Shepherd, The Lord's Prayer and Bless the Lord, O My Soul

Henry Thomas Hamblin

HAMBLIN
VISION
PUBLISHING

Hamblin Vision Publishing

Copyright

Contents

Introduction

BY NOEL RAINE, CHAIR OF THE HAMBLIN TRUST

H T Hamblin was a prolific author of a range of books, booklets and pamphlets offering practical advice on how to live in harmony with God, or what he sometimes referred to as *Source, the Universe,* or *the Cosmic*. However, this was not just a spiritual quest, or an attempt to avoid the troubles and cares of everyday life – far from it, for Hamblin was a very practical mystic – but a practical guide to each one to follow to increase health, happiness, and prosperity.

Hamblin founded the *Science of Thought Institute*, offering a course of practical lessons intended to guide his many thousands of students towards a happier, healthier and more prosperous life and, although he is sadly no longer with us in person, he left a wonderful legacy of publications that he had written from 1921 up to the time of his death in 1958. Some of those are still in print and available from **The Hamblin Trust** on www.thehamblinvision.org.uk but many have since gone out of print.

Conscious that the Trust will not be around forever, the custodians of Hamblin's teachings, the trustees of the Hamblin Trust, have decided to produce copies of Hamblin's earlier works in digital format to leave a legacy for future generations. Whilst the style of writing may now seem a little dated, Hamblin's teachings remain valid and, although edited a little to bring them more into line with current editorial style, we are pleased to bring to you in one compilation, three of Hamblin's earlier books offering a guide to a deeper, happier and joy-filled life:

- The Lord is My Shepherd (First published in 1935)

- Bless the Lord, O My Soul (First published in 1936)

- The Lord's Prayer (First published in 1937)

These are of course well-recognised writings in the Christian tradition. This is not surprising as Hamblin was essentially a Christian mystic, and his own spirituality was guided deeply by the simple words and teachings of Jesus. However, the three small books in this compilation offer Hamblin's personal insights on how they can be used to transform our lives, both spirituality and practically, leading to greater health, happiness, and joy. Indeed, the supporting text to the titles indicate their practical application:

- The Lord is My Shepherd: '*A study of Psalm 23 as a basis for the practice of affirmative prayer*'.

- The Lord's Prayer: '*A suggested amplification for dai-*

ly use'.

- Bless the Lord, O My Soul: '*Being some thoughts suggested by Psalm 103*'

It is our hope that this compilation will, indeed, help **you** to achieve the health and happiness that the application of Hamblin's teachings can provide and the sheer joy that arises from living in accordance with the simple spiritual insights he shares.

Many blessings for health, harmony and joy.

Noel Raine
Chair of the trustees
The Hamblin Trust

Concise Biography of Henry Thomas Hamblin

BY JOHN DELAFIELD, HAMBLIN'S GRANDSON

Who was Henry Thomas Hamblin?

Henry Thomas Hamblin was a spiritual teacher and writer based in Sussex, England, whose message and vision were straightforward and pragmatic. He believed that the spiritual life and the practical, everyday life were inseparable. His teachings centred around the power of thought and the importance of meditation to draw on the inner power, wisdom and love that we all have deep within us. Hamblin referred to this as "the Secret Place of the Most High" in the days before meditation was widely practiced in the West.

Hamblin was colloquially known as HTH, and later 'The Saint of Sussex'. Whilst his teachings leaned towards esoteric Christianity, his philosophy was truly universal, embracing the truths of all faiths. The emphasis of his message is on finding the power of spirituality within us all, in the context of our everyday lives, rather than religion. As a young man, he reacted against the dogma of his strict, religious upbringing, and believed that religion often divided people, while spirituality united people. His teachings came from a place of pure empathy and compassion for humankind.

Henry Thomas Hamblin worked right up to the end of his life in 1958 and left a legacy that continues to this day, its voice as much needed now as it ever was.

A Wayward Child

Henry Thomas Hamblin was born in 1873 in Walworth, South East London, of Kentish parents, and was the second of two sons. His father was very religious, and his grandfather a minister of the Baptist Church. His mother, although of diminutive size, was reportedly "great of soul" and ruled the family with benevolent autocracy. The family was poor, very poor, like all those living around them in that district of London in the late Victorian era, and, despite their hard work, the only education that could be afforded for Henry was an elementary one. He followed this with a course in technology, which proved to be of inestimable value to a youth who was considered by his parents and teachers to be wayward.

"Unstable as water; thou shall not excel," his mother reproached him regularly. No doubt she intended it to shame her son into a regime of self-improvement, in keeping with child-rearing practices of the time, but it was hardly confidence-inspiring! "Slacker!" was the repeated insult from his elder brother. Wiser, more objective, heads might have paused for long enough to recognise a certain potential in the young boy who, at the age of nine, could attempt the writing of a school newspaper. He had also established himself as something of an elocutionist. Writing and speaking would both prove valuable skills in later life.

His adolescent years gave little indication of an error in the family verdict. "Henry the wayward" moved from one poorly paid post to another, idled in between dead-end jobs, succumbed to bouts of ill-health, and, before he had reached the age of eighteen, had displayed more than the usual "adolescent failings", according to his autobiography, *The Story of My Life*. From a modern perspective, all these Victorian euphemisms point to Hamblin being something of a "bad lad", an impression added to by his own heavy hints that he had been no stranger to drinking and carousing. He suffered terribly from pangs of regret following his periods of over-indulgence, so that "Henry the sinner" became "Henry the saint" – until the next time. His pronounced rebellious streak landed him in hot water more than once. He constantly pushed against the boundaries of the fire-and-brimstone brand of Christianity in which he had been raised, which he felt to be unbearably restrictive. Reading about his struggles with authority as a young man somehow makes the rather aloof spiritual writer he became more accessible and endearing; it's hard not to warm to someone who so openly confesses their own faults and shortcomings, especially in the tightly buttoned-up era in which he lived. He was inspired by books, many of which fired his worldly ambition and prompted his spiritual imagination.

What his parents and educators overlooked was that Hamblin was a young man with huge aspiration, flushed with a youthful zest for life, and inspired by a worthy ambition to rise above the rut of his circumstances. Although he pushed against his father's dogmatic and punitive style of practising religion, at heart, he was deeply religious. A person's early environment, education, and adolescent behaviour can often determine the course of their life. Youthful indulgences of one sort or another are inevitable. Hamblin's studies of the New Testament, which revealed that selfishness and hypocrisy, rather than indulgence, received greater condemnation by Jesus, would have been very much in his consciousness.

A Successful Businessman

There is no doubt that Hamblin had an enquiring mind, and this, coupled with a desire for scientific accuracy, enabled him to achieve success in his later endeavours in business. In this, despite his lack of education, he was bolstered by boundless faith and courage, which, coupled with a shrewd business sense, ensured that he succeeded beyond all expectation. In 1898, having taught himself opthalmics at night, he qualified as an optician and set up his first successful business as an optician, Theodore Hamblin (now Dolland and Aitchison), frequented by royalty, the rich and the famous.

Hamblin was a natural entrepreneur and a born risk-taker. By this time, he was also a family man. He married Eva Elizabeth in 1902, and they went on to have two sons and a daughter.

He enjoyed acquiring several businesses, all with insufficient capital, and relying on credit and goodwill. He took more pleasure in the thrill of the challenge than in the promise of monetary gain. Far from being downcast in the face of numerous setbacks, he thrived on negotiating obstacles which appeared insurmountable. As soon as the business was established and running smoothly, however, rather than being satisfied with financial security and the ability to provide for his family, Hamblin's interest started to wane. He felt a loss of the initial drive and motivation, his physical and mental health began to decline... until the next big idea came along and away he would charge again, all fired up and raring to go.

Throughout all his wild days of youth and high-risk business ventures, Hamblin felt a great tug towards discovering a deeper meaning to life, beyond that of the daily struggle to make ends meet. Propelled by his discontent, he became a driven seeker after truth. In his quest, he met other prominent thinkers of the time and formed lasting friendships.

As his business success grew, so did a gnawing sense of depression. It was as if there was something inside him that had not yet found a voice. Around this time, he discovered the New Thought movement and began to read their publications. Hamblin realised then that none of his worldly success had made him happy. He felt that a move from London to the coast would be beneficial. Shortly afterwards came the outbreak of the First World War, and Hamblin went off to serve his country, leaving his business in the care of others, almost with a sense of gleeful relief, strange though it sounds.

But it was the sudden and unexpected death of his younger son at the age of ten, in 1918, that brought him to rock bottom and to question everything.

A Very Practical Mystic

Hamblin was not a genius, and millions of other people have made good in the world with even less promising assets. But it was in the second half of his life, when Hamblin turned away from creating highly successful business enterprises to focus instead on the spiritual realm, that his unique combination of the pragmatic and the profoundly spiritual shone forth. He has sometimes been described as a very practical mystic.

Hamblin began writing in the 1920s. The words seemed to flow from him. He found that writing clarified his thoughts. One of his first books written in this new phase of his career was *Within You Is The Power*, which was to sell over 200,000 copies. Other books soon followed. Hamblin believed that there is a source of abundance which, when contacted, could change a person's entire life. As long as people blamed their external circumstances for any misfortune, they were stuck in the 'victim role'; but if they moved in harmony with their inner source, their life could be full of abundance and harmony.

Soon after this, Hamblin set up a magazine called *The Science of Thought Review*, based on the principles of Applied Right Thinking. He wasn't discouraged by the fact that he had no experience of editing or publishing. His experience had taught him that if the mind worked in harmony with the Divine, then everything you needed flowed towards you. Anyone with any business sense at all knew that to set up a magazine with a first print run of 10,000 copies would be a risky thing to do. But Hamblin was not risk averse, to put it mildly! He wanted to put what he believed into practice. The only magazine of its kind in the 1920s, it soon gained a worldwide readership. Among his friends and contemporaries that were to contribute to the magazine were Joel Goldsmith, Henry Victor Morgan, Graham Ikin, Clare Cameron and Derek Neville, all of them prolific and successful writers. Apart from his international subscribers, Hamblin had close ties to comparative spiritual thinkers in many other countries, especially in the U.S.

Although he had been brought up in a strictly religious family, he hadn't found any of the answers he sought in the Church. He realised that, rather than following any creed or dogma, which didn't work for him anyway, he had to look within himself. He found contact with 'Presence' and realised it held the key to the peace he was seeking. All the time, his search was leading him nearer to discovering the way his thoughts affected his performance and outlook.

During the General Strike of 1926, the Great Depression of 1929-32, and again in years after the end of the Second World War, many homeless, unemployed wayfarers came to the Hamblin household seeking relief and shelter. Henry and Elizabeth provided them with a simple meal, new boots and clothing, and money for the road. Known colloquially as 'The Saint of Sussex", Hamblin was a man who applied his spiritual principles to his everyday life. Practical Mysticism was Hamblin's life's work. He helped people in deeply practical ways to become less fearful, happier, and more successful in their lives. To this end, he wrote books like *The Antidote to Worry*. However, later in life he realised that whilst these books genuinely helped people, they were largely concerned with the personality. He then wished to go a step further and become more fully a truly 'practical mystic', so he wrote a spiritual course of 26 lessons, each with a definite theme presented in a systematic way. This was designed to move beyond the constraints of personality so that the soul could breathe the pure air of Spirit. What was needed, he felt, was 'a total surrender of ourselves to the Divine.' The course is available as the book *The Way of the Practical Mystic.*

The Power of Thought

Hamblin was at the forefront of the New Thought movement which was gaining pace in the early 20th century. He discovered that 'new thought' was, in fact, ancient wisdom, based upon the truth that has always existed since before time began. All great souls give voice to that timeless truth in a myriad of different ways. Hamblin urges us to "Think in harmony with the Universal Mind." In other words, he underlines the fact that truth is and cannot be changed depending upon our mood or our whim.

Hamblin realised that we need not only a positive frame of mind but an applied way of thinking - Right Thinking, as he termed it. What did he mean by that? Well, he wrote a book on it, *The Little Book of Right Thinking*, which is in its 17th reprint. Essentially, he defines Right Thinking as:

- Thinking from the Divine standpoint.

- Controlling the thoughts so they do not go off on negative tangents away from the Divine Truth, which is always positive.

- Replacing negative thoughts with positive thoughts

- Living in the consciousness that all is well; and as an adjunct to this, remembering that perfection exists as a reality now, and to think in the consciousness of that knowledge.

- Meditation or prayer is the highest form of Right Thinking.

- Ultimately, however, the aim is to get beyond thought, 'to enter ultimate Truth'.

He says, 'When we cease thinking, we glide out on the ocean of God's Peace. Thought brings us to the foot of the mountain after which we have to proceed by intuition'.

> *'Health, Wealth and Happiness. Isn't this some-thing we all want, either for ourselves or for those dear to us? And yet, how many of us are struggling*

to reach or hold such a goal for a sustained period
of time?'

Hamblin's teachings explain how we can achieve all of these things, not by hard work and striving but by a simple change of thought. *Within You is the Power* is one of his simple but profound statements, and the title of one of his books.

Hamblin was a prolific author and had many thousands of followers studying and benefiting from his teachings and courses until his death in 1958. The simple principles contained in those teachings are as relevant today as they were when he was alive, and can still help us to achieve health, prosperity and happiness if we apply them conscientiously.

He died in 1958 in Chichester Hospital. The Hamblin Trust exists to this day to propagate the legacy of his work.

The Relevance of his Teachings Today

Hamblin was, essentially, a Christian mystic, yet his ideas about the simplicity and clarity of presence seem incredibly contemporary. He believed that the source of all wisdom is within us and all around us, and that this is the fundamental reality; there is no separation, and we are all one. His message and advice to all who read his work is that it is for everyone and is in harmony with the aspiration of all good people throughout time. Hamblin believed that there can be no finite creed of an infinite faith. Moreover, he suggests that, when creeds appear, true faith can be constrained.

He cautioned that if you seek God in prayer, the corollary is that you must have faith in Him. He often stressed that no prayer goes unanswered, and, although you may not get the answer requested, your prayer will be answered in some form. God is around us and within us, and this is the fundamental reality. He made it clear that, although human organisations come and go, God's laws are eternal, and that God is the quintessence of love, wisdom, and harmony. He expresses the clear view that "Blessed are they who believe and yet have not seen". The knowledge that God is born within us is fundamental to our understanding, and only by the loss of self can God be found. At the point a person surrenders his or her 'self' to God, it is then that a re-birth takes place and one's real life in God begins.

Some may question this view and ask: "What is this but the core teachings of the many brands of Christianity?" In response, Hamblin's view was that modern Christianity is a heterogeneous compound of the teachings of Jesus interwoven with historic pagan-based doubts and fears, litanies, supplications and more, all of which are closely guarded by a priestly hierarchy. These were strong views, and Hamblin does not disparage those who found them uncomfortable, as he says that churches are necessary and helpful for those who are succoured by them. Hamblin had a lifelong rebellious streak where authority was concerned, and this included the strictures of the Church. Hamblin would sometimes say that the Truth of the message of Jesus was so often wrapped up in dogma and creed that its purity and simplicity were obscured.

In his teaching, he states that first comes purity of intention, reminding his readers that one cannot serve God and Mammon. Either you trust God completely or you hedge your bets by having worldly alliances and a healthy bank balance. He maintains that trying to achieve both will impair spiritual development. Secondly, an individual's dedication to following God's path will require great patience, perseverance, faith and courage; but in following this path, the individual will develop forbearance and good will. He adds that other life experiences will follow naturally and lead to a developing compassion, which will enable the individual to radiate the love of God.

Where should we place Hamblin in the long line of mystics, seekers and finders? Perhaps it is rather impertinent to pose the question some 65 years after his death, but it is surely relevant to consider this point as, by any measure, he was an extraordinary person.

Remember that he was born into a life of poverty and obscurity but, despite a very limited education, by superhuman efforts of his imagination, he rose to wealth and secured an esteemed position in life, while all the time being aware of another "self" within him, a spiritual self. Dramatically, in the middle part of his life, he surrendered his material successes to follow his wider calling as a disciple of God. In this later life, he did not subscribe to any specific creed or form of religion. He was no haloed saint in the traditional sense, but he would have said, "What I have done, or rather what has been done through me, can be done by any person in the world according to their gifts and personal faith".

The essence of this teaching is that the latent power of God lies within everyone.

John Delafield is the grandson of Henry Thomas Hamblin and a retired RAF pilot. The majority of his childhood was spent living with his grandparents, Henry Thomas and Elizabeth Eva Hamblin.

Part 1

The Lord is My Shepherd: A study of Psalm 23 as
a basis for the practice of affirmative prayer

Hamblin Vision Publishing

CHAPTER ONE

The Eternal Shepherd of Souls

*There is one Lord and He is the Eternal Shepherd
of Souls*

The Twenty-third Psalm has been a sheet-anchor to saints, and those who have been saints in the making, from time immemorial. It is helpful to the beginner in the way, it is even more helpful to those who are bearing the heat and the burden of the day, and it is equally helpful to those who are nearing the end of their journey.

No matter how little the aspirant may know of Divine truths, this Psalm can help him. On the other hand, no matter how advanced and experienced he may be, he can find in it inexhaustible reservoirs of strength and power, through meditating upon it.

The Twenty-third Psalm is powerful because it is affirmative prayer in its most perfect form. Affirmative prayer is the stating of that which is eternally true of God, as the lover and shepherd of souls, and about each child of God, forever loved and cared for. Therefore, when we pray affirmatively, we declare the truth about God, and the truth about ourselves as the offspring of God. The result of this is that we become strengthened and established in God, because, through declaring Truth, all error is eliminated, for Truth is the only reality.

People often ask, "What is Truth?" It is impossible for any man to describe or define Truth, but the one who meditates daily upon God's word enters into Truth, in due course, and then he not only knows the Truth which makes men free, but also actually that he himself is being changed into its likeness. For it is an eternal truth that we become that which we contemplate.

Praying Affirmatively

People also ask, "How can I pray affirmatively, and positively?" The answer is, "Follow or copy the Twenty-third Psalm". "But what about the model prayer given by Lord Jesus?" it may be asked. The answer to this is that this is prayer of a different kind. I call it a prayer of invocation; but by "invocation" I do not mean supplication, but rather the use of creative words, or words which release and set in motion creative forces. In the beginning God said, "Let there be light, and there was light". In a similar way we're told to say, "Thy Kingdom come"; which really is like saying, "*Let* Thy Kingdom come".

We have, therefore, the two forms of prayer, and it is necessary to use both; but in this little work I wish to say a few words about the Twenty-third Psalm, the perfect model of affirmative prayer.

But this Psalm is far more than a model form of affirmative prayer. It also shows us the Path of Life, or Liberation, as it is sometimes called. In the Twenty-third Psalm we find described the three great stages of attainment through which every aspirant has to pass. The first stage is described in the first three verses, the second stage in the fourth verse, and the third stage in the concluding verses of the Psalm.

In the first three verses we find described in happy and felicitous language the blessed state of the beginner in the new life of the Spirit. Here we are shown the blessed state of one who has given his heart wholly to the Lord and whose one desire is that the Lord should lead him and guide him, withersoever He wilt.

In the fourth verse is described the difficult period of trial and stress in which we are proved and tested, and when the soul is subjected to perils and dangers, onslaughts and assaults which would overwhelm it, but for the protecting presence of the LORD, the Shepherd of souls.

The final verses (five and six) describe the happy and victorious state of those who have attained, i.e. Those who have won through to the rest that remaineth to the people of God, and which they have reached, not through their own struggles and conflict, although these have been many and faithful, but because the Lord has fought for them.

Some people do not agree with this view. They think that the first three verses describe the regenerative life, and that the fourth verse refers to physical death, and that verses five and six describe the Heavenly state experienced after death has been passed. I do not want to destroy the comfort that anyone may derive from this interpretation. It can certainly be taken to mean this, and those who wish to do so, are entitled to get what comfort they can from such an interpretation; but it is only a surface or partly true meaning, and therefore is not the wholly true one. The true interpretation, as is always the case, lies beneath the surface, and is found only as a result of searching, seeking and inward illumination.

On the other hand, there are those who look upon the Twenty-third Psalm as referring only to material supply. They think that all that it means is that the Lord will feed them and supply their temporal needs. It does mean this, of course, but it also means far more. When a child is adopted by earthly parents it is not merely fed, clothed, housed and given pocket money, but (as a rule, thank God) it is also loved, cherished, taught, instructed, guided, developed; and through all this loving care is made a good citizen, fit to occupy an honourable position in life. If this is true of earthly life, which is only an imperfect reflection of our real life in God, how much more true is it that the Twenty-third Psalm describes something far more wonderful and glorious than the mere supplying of our daily needs, important though these may be.

The Twenty-third Psalm describes the greatest thing in Heaven and earth - the regeneration of man, his rise from man to Man.

Now, let us inquire more minutely into this wonderful Psalm, considering it verse by verse; remembering, however, that we cannot understand Truth intellectually but that we can enter into a realisation of it, and this is the work of the Spirit of Truth who reveals Truth to us from within, through the awakening and quickening of an inward spiritual faculty, the while we reflect and meditate on the Divine word.

Verse 1: The Lord is my Shepherd

We need not enter into an intellectual explanation of the term LORD, or Jehovah, or Yahweh, as it should be; for I find that such explanations do not help us to realise the Truth, and thus really to *know* the LORD. It means to me that aspect of Deity that is loving and mighty, intimately interested in the affairs of man and the soul of man. In other words, the Shepherd of men and the Shepherd of souls. It is the same idea of God as that which St. John described as the Logos. That which was *with* God at the beginning, and yet was God. The Logos is God yet is something more than just Deity. The Logos is God made accessible to man; indeed, "in him was life, and the life was the light of men".

The term Lord to us means the Supreme, in His love aspect, intimately concerned in our affairs, whose greatest desire is that we should be brought out of darkness into His most marvellous Light.

We all have aspirations after God, the Supreme Good, and purity, wisdom, love and all the Divine qualities, and yet who is beyond and above all these. The great longing of our soul is to find God, and to be united with Him for ever; but it is the Lord who has placed the desire in our soul. God, as LORD, has only one desire, and that is to save man, or regenerate him, and turn him into the same likeness and substance as Himself.

The Path of Liberation

This can be accomplished only by man undertaking a journey and passing through certain experiences. Through these experiences he becomes changed in character and substance until he attains to a state of Divine union. But man cannot accomplish this of himself. Those who attempt to do so meet with disaster, for they cannot of themselves regenerate themselves. It is like a man trying to hoist himself in the air by pulling at his own shoelaces. Neither can he overcome the powers of evil that oppose him.

In order for man to become like unto God, i.e., a son of God, God has to stoop down and help him to attain. He does this as LORD. He thus becomes our Shepherd or Saviour. Without the Shepherd of our souls, we are indeed helpless and lost. But with His guidance and aid we are led through all life's experiences, kept from falling, and presented faultless before His presence with exceeding joy.

The lower can never raise itself to the higher. It is necessary for the Higher to stoop down and raise the lower to Itself. What a wonderful revelation of God is this, that He becomes the Lord, the Shepherd of our souls! God, the Infinite and

Eternal, the Supreme Power, Might and Majesty, whose Purity and Holiness are such as would destroy us if we approached Him in our unregenerate selves, stoops down and becomes our Shepherd and Guide. How wonderful!

The Lord of Heaven and earth, infinite in might and power, wisdom, knowledge, intelligence and every quality and virtue, is our Shepherd. Of whom, then, shall we be afraid? Shall we fear any experience that life can bring us? If God be for us, who, then, can be against us? "The Lord is my Shepherd". How wonderful!

It is not in the Twenty-third Psalm alone that this beautiful idea of the love aspect of Deity being our Shepherd is to be found. In Isaiah, chapter 40, verse 11, we find this lovely passage:

> He shall feed his flock like a shepherd;
> he shall gather the lambs with his arm,
> and carry them in his bosom,
> and shall gently lead them that are with young.

Also, the Lord Jesus said:

> I am the Good Shepherd, and am known of mine
> - and I lay down my life for the sheep.

This idea or doctrine of the Lord as Shepherd is not confined to the Bible. We find it in *The Divine Pymander of Hermes Trismegistus:*

> Pymander means 'Shepherd of men'.
> He is Leader and Teacher,
> Illuminator and Ideal archetype of all mankind.

How lovely it is to reflect on the fact that the Lord has been the Shepherd of souls all through the ages, and that we are all for ever kept in the love of God.

I Shall Not Want

Because the Lord is my Shepherd it is quite impossible for me to lack any good thing.

> The young lions do lack and suffer hunger;
> but they that seek the Lord shall not want any
> good thing.

In the Lord "dwelleth all the fulness of the Godhead, bodily". God is the only Substance. What appears to the senses as substance is not so really. Its only substantiality is due to the fact that it is supported by God, the only true Substance. Take away this support, matter, or what the senses regard as substance, at once would disappear. We can never lack any good thing the while we recognise, acknowledge, and realise this great truth that God is the only true Substance, that is eternally everywhere present, as the only Reality, underlying and upholding everything. The phenomenon which man calls form has no reality of its own. It exists only so long as it is supported by the true Substance and only Reality, God. One who recognises this great truth, and sees behind all appearance and form the one Substance and Reality, God, can never lack any good thing.

> Every good gift, and every perfect gift is from above, and cometh down from the Father of Lights, with whom is no variableness neither shadow of turning.
>
> James, 1:17

And so we state what is eternally true about the Lord, and eternally true about our true state, as recipients of Divine blessing: "The Lord is my Shepherd, I shall not want".

Elsewhere, I have stated that the object of the Psalms is to produce an effect on the mind. Their object is to bring us into a state of awareness or inward understanding, in which we really know the Truth in such a way that we are made free. In this psalm it is brought about by a combination of denials and affirmations. The affirmations greatly outnumber the denials, however. There are only two denials, while there are twelve affirmations.

In what is termed by some mental science the denial is generally put first. In this psalm it is put second. This, doubtless, is
the best place for it, for it sounds less effective if placed first,
such as:

> I shall not want,
> Because the Lord is my Shepherd.

But in the ordinary course of things, we generally put the
denial first. If we hear something said which is untrue, we
immediately deny it. "So-and-so is dead", we are told. But,
because we know that So-and-so is alive, we say "No, he is not
dead". After that we explain that we have seen him and spoken
with him only a few minutes before. Again, a child is afraid of
the dark, so we say at once that there is nothing of which to be
afraid. This is the denial. Then we go on to explain why there
is nothing to fear. This is the affirmation.

If our soul is in a state of fear, then we treat it like a child,
and deny that there is anything to fear, and then proceed to
affirm the truth about being supported by invisible powers and
upheld by the Everlasting Arms.

In the Twenty-third Psalm a similar procedure is followed,
except that the denial is placed second. The object of this is
to produce an effect on the mind. Usually, our mind works in
a material groove. It thinks round a central idea of privation.
Without knowing it, we think as though we were outside the
love and care of God. We think, inwardly and unconsciously,

that we are perpetually in a state of privation, and that we stand in need of things. Thus, we think in terms of evil, which is a state of privation - a deprivation of the good.

In the face of this appalling state of wrong thinking the truth is ejaculated, or thrown like a bomb into the very centre of our error and sense of separation:

The Lord is my Shepherd; I shall not want.

The object of this is to cause, as it were, an explosion, so as to break down, or split in pieces, the hard shell of error which wrong thinking has built up, and to destroy the set grooves of evil thought-habit, which are alien to God and Truth. The object aimed at is to bring us back from error to Truth. In the ordinary way, our subconscious thinking only too often runs something like the following:

I am friendless and alone, and God seems afar off. I have to fight for myself and look after self, otherwise, I am pushed to the wall. Life is unfriendly, and at any moment a great disaster may overtake me.

Although I may be able to keep going while health and strength last, yet if I become ill, or when I become old, I shall be thrown on the scrapheap. Enemies on every hand are plotting my downfall and evil powers seek to devour my soul.

At any moment some evil may befall me; I may lose my job, or be landed in a legal action, or an expensive operation, or be accused of a crime of which I am innocent, or something dreadful may happen to my loved ones.

The happiness that I have may at any moment be snatched from me. If such a thing did happen, then what should I do?

And so on.

In the face of all this, we are told to declare, and, by so doing, to tell our soul that "The Lord is my Shepherd, I shall not want".

Such a statement acts like a charge of dynamite. It blows into pieces the framework of our pessimistic thought-habit. It knocks all our worldly-wise, fearful, selfish philosophy into fragments. It declares that, instead of our being friendless and alone and at enmity with life and our fellows, at any moment liable to become the victim of evil happening and circum-stance, and, also, instead of our having to fight our fellow men for the prizes or even the necessities of life, like dogs fighting over a bone or wolves or rats over the dead body of one of their own kind; in the face of all this, it declares that the Lord, the Infinite and One Power, Intelligence, Wisdom, of the Universe, is Love, and that He is looking after us, even as an Eastern shepherd looks after his sheep.

The difference is staggering. It is an entire and complete reversal of all our natural ideas; it throws down the gauntlet to all the instincts of the race mind and the sophistries of the world.

To challenge the deeply entrenched powers of race-thoughts by the use of a simple statement of Truth such as this, is like little David going out to meet Goliath. He must have looked very pitiful going out alone with only a sling and stone to meet the heavily armed giant of the Philistines. To his enemies he must have even looked ridiculous. But he won easily, because he had such faith and confidence in God that he was inspired by a superhuman intensity of power and skill. In the same way, this little statement of Truth, "The Lord is my Shepherd", rends and disintegrates the power of established error, simply because it is Truth. For the reason that Truth is the only reality, and because it is the only thing that is real, it therefore must always win, when it is declared boldly in the face of that which is not Truth, and which, therefore, is not real, and which has no substance.

The only power that race-mind error possesses is the power we endow it by our thought, by our fear, and by our acknowledgement of it as truth, substance, and reality. When we refuse to accept or acknowledge the race-thought declaring in its stead the truth about the LORD, then the power of error is broken, for, being a lie or a no-thing, it has no reality. When we refuse to acknowledge error as truth, then it ceases to have power because we have put it out of our mind. If our mind is filled with the truth about God, and also the truth about ourselves, as children of God, forever loved and cared for, then error and evil and fear can have no place in our mind, and consequently are excluded from our life, our world, our universe.

The Psalm, therefore, starts off with the Centre and secret of the whole mystery.

> The Lord is the Supreme Good,
> the Essence of Goodness.
> All good comes, therefore,
> from the Lord, and from Him alone.

We, ourselves, have nothing, and, of ourselves, are nothing, but as the object of the Lord's love and care, we have everything. As a dearly loved child of God we are the recipients of every possible blessing, but of ourselves we possess nothing and are nothing. But, because the Lord is our Shepherd, we cannot want.

There is conflict within us until we learn to exalt the Lord, so that He can arise in us and reign in us and work His perfect will through us. Divine union is achieved through our will being attuned and made one with the will of the Whole. Then we come into harmony with the whole universe, and all conflict ceases.

The lesson to be learnt from all this is that we should daily and hourly acknowledge that all good comes from the Lord, who is infinite in might, power, wisdom and love; that the Lord is our Shepherd, and that because of His love we possess all things.

If we desire that all our temporal needs should be supplied in a perfectly harmonious fashion, then we must acknowledge at all times that we are supported by the Lord, and that we depend entirely on the blessing of the Lord. If we desire that the great longing of our soul should be satisfied, and that we should find God and live our life in him, then we must acknowledge that only the Lord our Shepherd can lead us to the consummation of all our hopes.

Do we desire that we be brought victoriously through all the great crises of life and to final attainment? Then we must put the Lord first, at all times, and ourselves only as the objects of Divine love and care. Through becoming nothing ourselves we become filled with the fullness of God.

Do we need instruction in Divine things? Then, if we look to the Lord, whatever we need for our instruction comes to us just at the right moment. The Lord is indeed our Shepherd, and we can never want.

CHAPTER TWO

I Shall Not Want

A t the risk of repeating myself, may I emphasise this: that Truth has no power in our life if we do not make use of it. We have to enter into it, and it has to enter into us, before it can become real to us, and a part of our life. An intellectual understanding of, or assent to, Truth does not bring its power into our life. Neither do affirmations of themselves. They are but the externals, so to speak. They are the preliminaries or the stepping stones. They are not the thing itself. We have to enter into the very heart of Truth, before it can become Truth to us, and the power in our life. It is true of course that we have to affirm Truth. The Twenty-third Psalm is an affirmation from its beginning to its end; but, merely affirming Truth is insufficient, if it does not lead to an inward realisation.

Thus, we might go on for years, reading or repeating the Twenty-third Psalm daily, in an exterior and intellectual kind of way, and yet nothing might be achieved, for the simple reason that we have not approached any nearer to the heart of Reality. If we would discover Truth interiorly, we must seek interiorly. We have to withdraw from outward things and sense excitements, and from external thought, and then seek inwardly for hidden depths, powers and understanding. Then in the quietness we can say:

> The Lord is my Shepherd;
> I shall not want.

When we seek interiorly, we reach, so to speak, to the heart of God; we cease dealing with externals and effects, and instead make contact with the Cause of things. When we reach the Secret Place of Power, it becomes possible for us to set in motion the Immense Powers and Potencies of the One Source of all Power, Life, Energy, and Intelligence. When we reach the Centre of Life and Power, and declare, "the Lord is my Shepherd, I shall not want", such a statement has power; it sets in motion the greatest powers, or rather, the One Power in the Universe. Yet paradoxically, it is through using such an affirmation that we reach an understanding in which we touch Reality. But it must be declared interiorly, as it were, with the heart. Then it becomes possible for us to find the Secret Place. When we understand interiorly - that is, when we enter into a state of awareness, or knowledge by the soul - that "The Lord is my Shepherd, I shall not want", so great is the Power that is set in motion, it does not matter how alarming may be the appearance of lack, nor how hopeless our position, deliverance is a foregone conclusion.

Working Miracles

It needs insight to understand Truth, and faith to stick to it, and to persevere unafraid until victory is achieved and the promises of God vindicated. Many wonder how miracles are achieved. A miracle is the bringing about of something that, humanly speaking, is impossible. It is achieved by realising its possibility in God, by declaring it and affirming what we know interiorly to be true and taking our stand in the truth that we have declared; after which we have to stick to it, in spite of apparent defeat, failure and every kind of discouragement.

At the present moment we may not be able to see how our various lacks can possibly be overcome. These may be of a material nature, or of a spiritual kind, but in either case the outlook may look dark and completely hopeless. We may lack means, or health, or friends, or guidance, or spiritual light; humanly speaking we may be on the brink of ruin; we may be bankrupt of health; we may be sunken so deep in spiritual darkness, that there may seem to be no hope for us. Yet, if we meet our state of lack with an interior realisation of the truth of the whole matter, and with a firm declaration of "The Lord is my Shepherd, I shall not want", and if we take our stand in what we have declared, and stick to it, even though the heavens fall, then our lack must be supplied.

> The young lions do lack and suffer hunger; but
> they that seek the Lord shall not lack any good
> thing.

The term "young lions" refers to the outward man, who relies on the arm of flesh. Those who "seek the Lord" are they who find God interiorly, in the Secret Place, and they discover the Source and satisfaction of all their need.

The Psalm of the Inward Power

The Twenty-third Psalm is generally regarded as a psalm of peace and quietude. It is, but it is much more. It teaches stillness, but it also teaches the power of stillness. It shows us how to reach the Centre and Source of all power. It shows us how to reach that point of balance which has been known by all the great seers and prophets all down the ages, and which was the cause of their wonder-working, and the source of their power.

The great secret is balance. The sun and its planets, the moon and the stars are all balanced in space. Because they obey, perfectly, natural law, they are always at the point of balance. There is no conflict. The conflict of opposing forces ceases when the object attracted or repelled reaches its true state of balance or poise. There can never be any conflict, or disorder, or strain or struggle, at the point of balance. A heavenly body is always in its right place, at the right moment, and is always doing its right work, or fulfilling its true destiny, simply because it is always in a state of balance. It does not struggle to go here or there; it does not fight against this or that force. It allows each law and power or force to operate and bring it to a middle or neutral point, a point of balance, and, consequently, effortless achievement.

The Centre of Power

We thus see in the natural universe an outward reflection of the hidden mystery which some describe as "mystical action in inaction". There is a point in consciousness where all conflict ceases, and where the pairs of opposites reach a point of balance. When we reach this point the humanly impossible becomes Divinely possible.

The object of the Twenty-third Psalm is to bring us to this point of realisation of Truth, which was the hidden secret of the ancients, and today is the hidden secret which many are seeking. It was the hidden secret of the mystical side of alchemy, of the Philosopher's Stone, of the transmutation of base metal into gold. These were merely terms to hide the Truth, and thus to protect those who knew Truth from being persecuted and murdered by the orthodox religionists of their time.

The effect of meditating upon, and pondering over, the Twenty-third Psalm, with the windows of the soul open in a receptive attitude, waiting for the Spirit of Truth, Who is our only teacher, to reveal Truth to us from within, not through the Intellect, but direct to the soul, the effect of all this is to bring us into a state of awareness in which we know the real, true inwardness of things, the very heart of the truth as it is in the Mind of God.

The effect of declaring and meditating upon the words "the Lord is my Shepherd, I shall not want" is to bring us into a state, not merely of conscious immortality, but of something far greater, viz., our true identity as the offspring of God, abiding in Eternity, rooted and grounded in the Eternal and in a state of unity or at-one-ment with the Divine.

Perhaps I ought to correct myself by saying that this effect is brought about by meditation upon the whole psalm, combined with passing through those experiences described in the Psalm; for it has a two-fold message. It describes the path along which we have to travel, and also at the same time awakens our inward understanding.

Now, after all this digression let us return to an examination of the psalm, sentence by sentence, and idea by idea. The next sentence is:

"He maketh me to lie down in green pastures".

The Prayer Book version puts it, "He shall feed me in a green pasture". The marginal rendering gives, "He maketh me to lie down in pastures of tender grass". We are fed not on burnt-up pastures, but in green, well-watered grasslands, where the grass is luscious, and rich, and luxuriously satisfying. The Lord leads us to the rich green pastures of tender grass, where, when we are abundantly satisfied, we can lie down, and rest, with every possible need supplied abundantly and all our desires appeased.

God's Idea is Abundance

The Psalmist seems to be at pains to emphasise and impress upon us the fullness and richness and luxuriant abundance of the provision of Divine love. We are not led to a scanty pasture in arid lands, but to the richness of a green pasture where we can eat our fill of abundant and luscious herbage.

No longer do we have to search hungrily for such scanty food as a dry and thirsty land may provide; but we are plenteously fed and are made to lie down in the midst of an overflowing abundance.

The Psalmist, by a happy choice of language and a clever use of words, evidently desires to convey the idea not only of God's sufficiency, but of God's abundance. God never does things by halves; He is not niggardly or penurious; He overwhelms us with His love. We are given the same idea in the story of the prodigal son. Not bread in his father's house, and the position of an hireling, but the fatted calf, the robe, the ring, and the position of an accepted son of a rejoicing father. This is God's way of dealing with us.

True Substance

As we meditate upon this Truth-statement of the reality about God, it is as though we glide out into the Eternal, to find

ourselves established in God the only true Substance. We luxuriously stretch ourselves and lie down in the consciousness
that all good [spiritual, mental, moral, physical] is the reality,
and that we are one with [or in a state of union with] That
which changes not.

As the children or offspring of God, all our needs, both of
our soul and our body, have been supplied from before the
foundation of the world, and must continue so, eternally. For
the true Substance, God, is eternal, and we are, as it were, a
spark from the Divine flame. Even as in the acorn there lies
potentially a mighty oak tree, so are we, too, filled with mighty
potentialities. "It doth not yet appear what we shall be, but we
know that when He shall appear, we shall be like Him", the
Divine Archetypal Man who hath put all things under his feet.

Through meditating on this psalm [or upon other statements
of Divine Truth] we enter into a state of interior awareness,
in which we know that we are at one with the Cause and
Substance of things, and that we are not at one with the outer
shell of things which are only effects. The outer man is as the
grass of the field, which today is and tomorrow is cast into the
oven. We are not this outer shell at all, neither are we under the
domination of outward things, powerful though they be, on
their own plane; but we belong to the Eternal Cause, we are
one with That which changes not. St. Paul must have realised
this when he said, "For your life is hid with Christ in God".
It is not the outward man that is at one with the Eternal, for
the first man is of the earth, earthy; but the second is the Lord
from Heaven. It is the Heavenly man in us, and who is our real

Self, who is at one with the Eternal. "Christ in you the hope of glory", the Heavenly Man in us who connects us to the Eternal.

Temporal as well as Spiritual

Some readers at this point may express the doubt as to inward realisation being able to change the outward life. They cannot see how realising inwardly that one is a child of God, and that the real part of us is already in the Eternal and Unchanging Reality, can have any effect upon the outward life, or our circumstances and environment. The reason they cannot understand is because they look at life from a materialistic point of view. They think that outward things are real, solid and unalterable; consequently, it is impossible for the invisible, silent forces to alter them. As thousands know, a realisation of Truth and an inward adjustment to the Divine bring about great changes in the outward life. This can be explained in several different ways, but I cannot stop to explain them all.

Obviously, when our thinking is changed, we begin to see things in a different light. The outward life and material things, because they are merely transient reflections of the Real and Eternal, are all perverse, or seen in a wrong or inverted way. Man's ideas are the very opposite of Divine ideas; therefore, if man is to think with God he has to reverse his thinking entirely. The natural mind thinks that the outward life is real and concrete, while the eternal or invisible is vague and visionary. Actually, it is the other way about. As the late Sidney Klein, a scientific man, used to say: "The invisible is the Real, and the visible the unreal". The Invisible is the Cause; the visible is an effect. Because this is true, if we live in the consciousness of Truth, and are in union with the Power, Wisdom, Substance and Intelligence that upholds all things, then the perfection of Reality and the Divine Idea must tend to manifest outwardly.

Another Explanation

Again, metaphysicians say that the only thing that they can be certain of is consciousness. If this be true, then the disorder of life is due to our accepting suggestions of evil, which through being accepted, become real to us, and part of our life. In such a case, what we have to do, obviously is to refuse to accept suggestions of evil, so that they cannot become part of our life, and instead to make positive suggestions of good.

Of course, this is merely a way of explaining things, so that people should be able to lay hold of the idea of positive prayer. There are other ways of explaining matters, but they all refer to the same thing; it is only the language and illustration that differ.

How wonderfully does affirmative prayer, such as the Twenty-third Psalm, meet the case. If it is true that we are the victims of suggestions of evil, and what is needed is to refuse to accept such suggestions, so that it cannot become real to us, and part of our life; and if in its place we ought to make positive suggestions of good; if this is the case, then the Twenty-third Psalm is the very thing that meets the case.

Instead of our accepting suggestions of lack, we declare, "the Lord is my Shepherd, I shall not want". The denial "I shall not want" destroys the negative suggestion, while the affirmation "The Lord is my Shepherd" gives us the positive suggestion. If we bring the Lord into it, then suggestions of evil, of lack, of negative ills, are destroyed; so that instead of suggestions of evil and lack becoming real to us, and part of our life, the reality of God's Truth becomes truth to us and part of our life.

Faith and Knowing

But there are those who do not find such an explanation either helpful or necessary. They *know* that the Lord provides, and that He is able to raise up, and to cast us down. They know that the Lord is able to laugh at the might of kings and bring to nought the schemes of proud nations. One who knows the Lord in this way can never lack any good thing. The simple faith of a simple- minded believer in God, one who is willing to renounce his intellectual pride, and become as a little child, is more powerful and effective than all the philosophy that was ever expanded. A personal approach to the LORD, like the coming of a small child to its mother, is more effective than the weaving of subtle theories and explanations about God and life.

Indeed, the direct approach to God and Truth, not through intellect, but through becoming receptive to the Divine Spirit of Truth is the only way of reaching a state of inward realisation. Directly we start using our intellect or human mind we cease to be receptive to the inward revelation of Divine Truth. It is as though our soul had windows. If we can only keep these windows open, then we can see and understand Truth. But directly we try to find God through the human mind these windows become closed.

The way, therefore, to enter into an inward realisation of the truth of the Twenty-third Psalm is to get into a receptive state and repeat it, slowly, sentence by sentence. Paradoxically, the way to become receptive to its hidden truth is to repeat it, and dwell and reflect upon it.

Practical Application

When we are faced by a first class worry, or when something has upset us, we may find it impossible to concentrate our attention upon the words of the Psalm. Our mind is in a whirl, and our thoughts race round and round the idea of the thing that is troubling us. But, if we persevere in repeating over and over again, quietly and gently, yet firmly,

> The Lord is my Shepherd;
> I shall not want.
> He maketh me
> to lie down in green pastures

and so on, then in course of time, the mind begins to pay attention, and the thoughts become disciplined. Persisting in our efforts, we gradually become calm, and thoughts about the truth about God, and the truth about ourselves as children of God, forever loved and cared for, take the place of the worry or fear thoughts which have previously dominated us.

Our efforts are not directed towards understanding intellectually or even using the human mind at all. Indeed, our object is to calm and quiet and the natural mind so that the spiritual mind, which alone can discern spiritual and eternal truth, can function in its stead.

We cannot enter into an inward realisation by the soul if we try to understand by the use of the human mind. Thinking Truth [or as near as we can get to Truth] by the human mind is helpful up to a point, but beyond this point we cannot go, if we use the usual process of thinking. At this point we advance beyond human thought. Then, when the human mind ceases to interfere, the spiritual mind begins to act, and through being receptive to Divine ideas, functions in harmony with the Mind of God.

Wonder-Working

We can never work wonders or bring about things which the human mind regards as miracles through the intellect. The way of achievement and the path of power are found through knowing by the soul and feeling by the heart. One of our readers who has achieved wonders, on a microscopical income, and who has not only maintained herself, but has also been the means, in God's hands, of helping healing and supporting others, says that she never *feels* poor. This is the secret of her wonder-working powers. If she were to allow herself to *feel* poor, then her limitations and difficulties would rear themselves up, and tower above her, and she would be submerged. But she does not allow this to take place. She keeps her mind raised to the higher plane of consciousness, in which she *knows* and *feels* herself rich in God. She knows and feels that the Lord is her Shepherd, and that therefore she can never lack any good thing.

Feeling Rich in God

When one is without either money or prospects it is difficult not to feel poor and at the mercy of circumstances. The healing of such circumstances is, however, through a change of consciousness. When we are faced by appearances of lack, if we allow them to dominate us and tower above us, and if we fear them, and give them a measure of reality by acknowledging them as real, then they become real in our experience, and we become their slaves. If, however, we refuse to accept them in consciousness, and affirm that the Eternal God is our refuge, and that the Lord is our Shepherd, and so on, thus taking our stand in Truth, until we *know* and *feel* rich in God, then we become raised above our difficulties, so that instead of being dominated by them, we are able to put them under our feet. They lose their power over us when we realise that our life is lived in God, and that in God is no lack, and never can be, but only abundance of all possible good and substance.

Good Comes from One Source Only

The object of the Twenty-third Psalm is to bring us into this higher consciousness, in which we know that there is no lack, but only fullness and richness, in all needed things, both for the soul and the body. "God *is* a rewarder of them that diligently seek him". Our needs are many, and they vary with the individual, but whatever our need may be, it is abundantly supplied out of His riches in glory [the Higher Consciousness or Realm of Light]

From no other Source can they be supplied. All good must come from above. The lower cannot build up to the higher. Man can never produce the Divine. The Divine has to stoop down to man if he is to be lifted up out of his troubles and delivered from his weaknesses and limitations. Yet, paradoxically, man can never rise, if he remains below. He can live the life of victory and mastery only through becoming unified with That which never knew or knows defeat, and which transcends all human weaknesses, even as the mountain towers above the plain.

An Ant Crawling Amongst Mountains

Occasionally I receive letters from people who are in a state of domination by circumstances. Their troubles tower above them and blot out their sky. They are like an ant crawling amongst mountains. But not only do they allow their troubles to tower above them, they also pray to a God who is afar off.

They say: I keep on praying most earnestly for this trouble to be taken away, or for that thing to be done, or that something else may come to pass; but circumstances only become more difficult.

But such prayer is not affirmative; it has nothing in common with the Twenty-third Psalm. There is nothing in it that can raise their consciousness above their circumstances. It does not declare that which is eternally true of God, and every child of God. It does not raise those who pray to a state of *knowing* and *feeling* that all is well, and that their needs are eternally supplied, and that they are one with the true Eternal Substance of the universe. In spite of all their prayers, the mountains of trouble still tower above them; while God still seems as far off as ever.

But, when one makes use of affirmative prayer, such as the Twenty-third Psalm, one's feet become planted upon the rock of Truth, and the consciousness raised to the Reality, where neither fear, suggestion, nor lack, nor evil can enter.

The Fault is Not in Our Stars

More and more I am convinced that our outward life and circumstances are largely the outcome of our thought-habit and mental attitude. More and more am I convinced of the truth of Shakespeare's words: "The fault, dear Brutus, is not in our stars, but in ourselves, that we are underlings". If we believe that we are the victims of circumstance, or our unlucky star, then we are victims and prisoners. We lay ourselves open to negative influences; indeed, we invite them.

It is not easy, however, for us to accept this truth, and to realise it when placed in a very difficult position of lack. If we are out of employment, and everybody "turns us down", and we receive harsh treatment, or callous indifference everywhere, we are apt to become not only discouraged, but actually resentful. If, however, we allow these moods to overcome us, then we make our life far more difficult, and we also drive all good away from ourselves. But, if we can only overcome our discouragement and depression, and turn resentment into forgiveness and goodwill, the things become much easier for us. And if, in addition, we enter into the Spirit of the Twenty-third Psalm, and realise its truth, then wonderful things become possible.

So long as we think that things are fixed and concrete and unalterable, they remain fixed and unalterable as far as we are concerned. If we think and acknowledge that we are the victim of a cruel industrial system, and that we can do nothing, but must simply wait for something to be done for us by others, we remain a victim. But when we take our stand in God and Truth all things become possible. A ready-made heaven does not, however, drop into our lap; but we may discover some new avenue of service in which we find happiness, freedom and self-expression. After which, of course, the supply of our needs follows as a natural course.

Practical Experience

People write to me sometimes sceptically asking, "have you ever known poverty?" Yes, I have. I started life without a penny, and for half my life had to struggle and battle with life's difficulties and trials. Therefore, I can appreciate how they feel about the apparent hopelessness of their position. But, I am afraid that so long as they maintain their present belief they will remain in bondage to circumstance. Our Lord said, "If Thou canst believe, all things are possible to him that believeth". Not *some* things, but *all* things are possible. The reverse of this is equally true. I am quite sure of this, that if I had adopted the type of mental attitude of those who write to me, I should have been in much the same position as they themselves are. Also, I know this, that if I had allowed discouragement to get the better of me, and resentment, and depression, then, by this time, I should probably have been in the workhouse, or something approaching it. I know this, also, that if I had allowed my mind to be fixed in the ideas of hopelessness and helplessness, lack and limitation, then my life would have by now become a complete expression of such ideas.

Of course, I gladly acknowledge that all good comes from the LORD. Without the Divine blessing no good can be achieved, but we need to adopt the right mental attitude, and to think in harmony with the Divine Mind, in order to make an opening, and provide a free passage through which the Divine blessing can manifest. Of ourselves, we can do nothing; but positive right thinking, as taught in the Twenty-third Psalm, makes it possible for good to manifest, and for us to be guided into a richer and fuller life.

I also acknowledge that there are certain big events, or crises of life which probably cannot be averted. But, if they come, or when they come, a right attitude of mind, and a realisation of Truth, are our greatest defence. If, when faced by a great crisis, we get to work on the Twenty-third Psalm, and realise it and live in it, then either the great thing that faces us dissolves away or else we find it is a great blessing. In any case we gain strength and wisdom with which to meet it, so as to turn seeming evil into good; whereas, without the aid of Truth, our reaction to the trouble would be wrong, and would therefore make matters far worse.

What is termed "right thinking" does not promise to make life a bed of roses, but taking our stand in God and Truth enables us to react to life's experiences in the right way, so that instead of being hindrances or causes of failure, they become stepping stones to higher things. Instead of going progressively downhill, we travel progressively uphill. Instead of slipping down, we climb up. Instead of becoming weaker, we become stronger.

No Inflation of Ego

In affirmative prayer, such as is outlined for us in the Twenty-third Psalm, there is no danger of inflating the self or personal ego. We are safe from ego inflation - which, if it takes place, effectively keeps us out of the Kingdom and from God

- because we are taught to put the Lord first. It is because the Lord is our Shepherd that all the wonderful things which are described in the Psalm are true. These great blessings and privileges are not ours because we deserve them, but because the Lord is taking care of us, in His great love. Sheep are stupid creatures, prone to wander and to follow other sheep when they go wrong; they also have no power of defence. Is not this true of us? How stupid we are, how dark our natural mind! How prone to wander and get ourselves into serious trouble! How defenceless we are, when attacked by evil powers, or old habits and temptations! But, because the Lord omnipotent is with us, and because of His mighty love, we are guided and led, sustained and supported, protected and preserved through all the experiences of life, until at last we come to the state of attainment in this life, promised us in the last verse of the Psalm.

CHAPTER THREE

The Waters of Quietness

When we enter into the same consciousness, or state of realisation, as that in which the writer of the Twenty-third Psalm was, when he wrote it, we enter into a state of peace, poise and power. Until this takes place the psalm and our meditation upon it are not Truth to us but are a way of approach to Truth. One who reads this, and who may not yet be able to enter into the higher consciousness, should not be discouraged, or think that he has failed. He has not failed; he has simply not yet arrived: but he is on the way; he is travelling the path. We cannot become adepts in a day. It takes time to accomplish the greatest thing possible in this life, viz., the finding of God, and entering into God-consciousness.

Newcomers are apt to be impatient. They think that the more books they can read, and the more lessons they can study, the more rapidly they will progress in understanding. The reverse actually is the case. So long as they are in a hurry, no progress, whatever, can be made. It is only when they give up all their hurry and mental excitement, and become leisurely and composed, and are content to learn and develop or unfold at the right speed (God's speed), that they make any progress at all. What they are seeking to achieve is the greatest of all achievements; and they are building far better than they know. They are endeavouring to accomplish something far greater than their wildest dreams have imagined; so that any progress, no matter how slow, or how small, is great and wonderful. We have to learn to put the brake on and to go slowly.

Waiting

I stay my haste, I make delays,
for what avails this eager pace!
I stand amid the eternal ways,
and what is mine shall know my face.

John Burroughs

Through meditating upon a portion of God's words, in the way we are doing with the Twenty-third Psalm, we reach the same consciousness as that of the one who wrote it. This is true even when we may not be able to understand intellectually what is written. Gradually there grows up within us a consciousness, or state of interior realisation or awareness, in which we know and feel [enjoy a state of awareness] the same as did the writer at the time he wrote the words upon which we meditate.

This is the great value of God's word; it reveals its hidden truth to us while we reflect and meditate upon it. At first, that upon which we meditate bristles with ideas and suggestive thoughts;

then, after a time, we pass beyond thought to a state that transcends human thinking to a state that is one of knowing inwardly, or of soul awareness.

While we meditate together, in this inquiry into the Twenty-third Psalm, I speak of the ideas and thoughts which are suggested to me, or which rise into consciousness, while so doing. But these in themselves are of no use, except insofar as they help to introduce us to a state of consciousness that is beyond and above ordinary thinking. These reflections and observations and amplifications in which I indulge are after all merely a kind of "natural mind" commentary; and consequently, they are not Truth, because no one can speak Truth, but only talk about it. It is true that what we want is not to talk about Truth, or to talk around it, but to deal with Truth itself. As, however, we have no language that can express Truth, and as the human mind is incapable of grasping Truth, we have to be satisfied with saying what it is not, and with using various illustrations from human life, or imperfect analogies, all of which help to bring the mind to a state of receptiveness towards Truth. This receptivity of the soul makes it possible for Truth to come to the soul by direct knowing. In spite of what we're doing, or as a result of it, the natural mind becomes still or calm, the "joyless quest of the human mind" ceases, and suddenly we enter into peace - the peace of God. The peace of God can be entered into only by the one who is attuned to it. Our object in meditating upon the Twenty-third Psalm is that we may become attuned to it, and by so doing, become attuned also to the mind of God.

Let us therefore proceed with our consideration of the Psalm, verse by verse.

He Leadeth Me Beside the Still Waters

The marginal rendering is "waters of quietness". The Prayer Book version gives "beside the waters of comfort". Although different, all these terms convey helpful suggestions to the soul.

Stillness

Be still and know that I am God.

The Lord leads me into a state of stillness. My mind, due to the Spirit's influence, is now like a calm lake, reflecting the heavens above. In a state of stillness, which is of God, my mind reflects the beauty and perfection of Divine Truth.

All worry and strain are gently laid aside.
Quietly and serenely,
I rest in the Father's love.
Through an inward stillness
I realise that I am loved and cared for.

And so I rest in the Stillness, away from the fever of life. I am in the calm and serenity of Heaven. I am in a state of oneness or at-one-ment with the peace of God.

Quietness

In quietness and in confidence shall be your strength.

Now in the Silence I find God in my own soul. All the hubbub of life is left behind. All its discordant noises are hushed, and now in the quietness and confidence of the Spirit I realise that I am rooted in the eternal, and that my "life is hid with Christ in God".

Comfort

The waters of comfort refresh my soul and fill me with new life and power. My thirsty soul is now satisfied in God. Because I am filled with all the fullness of God, I enjoy the comfort of having all my needs supplied in God.

Healing Distraught Minds

The psychological effect of contemplating still waters is to calm, compose and heal. A French specialist in nervous diseases used to make his patients who were suffering from nervous depletion and exhaustion to lie down for a certain time daily, and while so doing to gaze at a picture of a piece of water that was perfectly still. There was nothing in the picture but water and the setting sun. The light from the sun, which was near the horizon, was reflected in the water in the form of horizontal lines. There was nothing vertical in the picture. For instance, there were no masts of ships, for they would suggest work and activity. There were no trees fringing the water, for they would suggest uprising energy, reaching upwards, and so on. There were just the water and the horizontal rays of light, so that rest, repose, peace, relaxation should be suggested to the patient, the while he or she reclined at full length gazing at the picture of quietness. I have no doubt that the treatment was helpful and successful up to a point. Also, I know that most people would rather pay much money, even hundreds of pounds, for such treatment, than meditate upon the Twenty-third Psalm. But the Psalm, because it is God's word, will accomplish perfectly that which psychology can only achieve partially or imperfectly. Psychological methods are good, but spiritual methods are better, because they lead to a state of knowing, in which all fear passes away, and the soul rests quietly and happily in God.

Not Merely Quietness, but Inexhaustible Life

But it is not merely the quietness of the water that we have to consider, but also that which water itself typifies. Water stands for Eternal Life. It is the symbol of the Inexhaustible Life of God given to man. Jesus said to the woman of Samaria:

But whosoever drinketh of the water
that I shall give him shall never thirst;
but the water that I shall give him
shall be in him a well of water
springing up into everlasting Life.

The water that the Lord Jesus gives us is Living Water; it is the life of God made available for us, who of ourselves, and by ourselves, have no true life of our own. So Jesus, in His mercy and grace, brings us to the Living Waters of Quietness [Peace of God] and Comfort [Satisfaction and Fulness in God]. We become new creatures or beings, no longer feeding on the husks of worldly things, but upon the true Substance and Reality.

Now we must pass on to a consideration of the next verse. This is a very wonderful one indeed, but they are all wonderful. Here it is, or rather, the first part of it, for we must examine it in sections.

He (the Lord) restoreth my soul

"I will restore unto you the years which the locust hath eaten". How blessed was my soul, when I first discovered the truth of this promise, and realised that it referred to me, personally. What joy was mine when I knew that the Spirit was speaking about my own unprofitable life, with its wasted years. God is always forgiving, healing and restoring not only the wasted years [Oh, how great is His mercy!], but also our soul. He could not do otherwise, because of his nature and character. We see a reflection of this in the physical plane. When allowed to function normally Nature always heals us, and restores us, physically. If we cut our finger it heals up. If we break a limb, it joins together perfectly, if the bones are set correctly. If we make ourselves ill through overwork or overindulgence, Nature speedily restores us if we give up our wrongdoing and live normally. It is the same with our soul. God restores our soul, removes all its injuries and disfigurements and makes it whole again.

Nature, a Great Restorer

Some years ago, I used to cycle almost daily to a certain sandy beach on the shore of the English Channel. In those days one could walk along lovely sands for miles and see hardly a single person and do pretty well as one liked; but things are changed now. Even in those almost Eden-like days, however, there were times when the beach was invaded by charabanc loads of people and children from adjacent towns. Alas, they had not learned to behave. They were unacquainted with nature and ignorant of her orderly ways. They showed their disregard for all order and beauty by disfiguring the lovely beach and by scattering all over it their refuse and rubbish. No doubt the trippers had "a lovely time", although they did not stop to admire and enjoy the beauties around them, but they left the beach in a horrible state of disorder and ugliness.

But Nature is a great restorer. After the crowd had gone, the tide came creeping up. Slowly but irresistibly, it rose, until all the untidy, disfiguring works of man's disorder, together with his rubbish and refuse of empty tins, bottles, paper bags and whatnot, were covered. Then the waves pounded on that beach, and washed it clean and scoured it, and reshaped it. After which the moon arose, and there were beauty and quiet and peace, where but recently had been ugliness, noise and disorder. Then the tide went down again. And so, the next day, there was the beach completely restored again to its original beauty and order. It was as though man had never disfigured it, so perfect was the restoration that had been made. So beautiful was it that one walked gently upon its surface for fear of disturbing it or miring its loveliness and perfection of form.

God the Great Restorer of Souls

Yes, Nature is a great restorer. What I have described is an outward symbol of what takes place within. Our soul becomes disfigured and scarred, wounded and weakened, through contact with the world, and through conflict with sin and temptation. Its calm is disturbed, its form disfigured, its loveliness destroyed. But, because we turn to the Lord, and find Him in the Silence, "He restoreth our soul". The mighty ocean of God's Love and Power and Life submerges our soul and restores it to its perfect form. The injuries and wounds are healed, and even the scars are removed, so that our soul is made anew, even as Naaman's body was like unto the flesh of a little child, when he dipped himself seven times in the waters of Jordan.

God not only restores our soul in this way, but He also restores our soul, when it is faint and weak and weary, by imparting to it His own life and strength.

> He giveth power to the faint;
> unto them that have no might
> He increaseth strength.
> Even the youths shall faint and be weary,
> and the young men shall utterly fall:
> but they that wait upon the Lord shall renew
> their strength;
> they shall mount up with wings as eagles;
> they shall run and not be weary;
> they shall walk and not faint.

The youths and young men signify the strength of man at its best, but unsupported by spiritual power. They will fail in the day of trial; but those who turn to the Lord, and rest in the Silence, are strengthened by the power and might of the everlasting God, the creator of the ends of the earth, Who fainteth not, neither is weary.

The Lord gives power to our fainting soul. Because of our weak condition He is able to impart to our soul His own power and strength. Because we realise our own weakness and helplessness, we cast ourselves upon God so completely and utterly, and with such an abandon, that all dependence upon self and the arm of flesh is surrendered. Then it is possible for the Spirit of the Lord to enter our soul and to fill it with His life, wisdom, love and power. "He restoreth my soul".

To find God in the Silence, and to enter into the rest which God has prepared for us, is the remedy for every ill. When the activities of the natural mind are stilled, we get back to that point or state which was before our thinking and willing began.

As Jacob Boehme says in his *Dialogues of the Supersensual Life*:

> Son, when Thou art quiet and silent, then art Thou as God was before Nature and Creature, Thou art that which God then was; Thou art that whereof He made Thy nature and creature. Then Thou hearest and seest even that where-with God himself saw and heard in thee, before ever thine own willing and thine own seeing be-gan.

In the Silence we get right back to the point where our contrary will and false imagination arose. Therefore, it becomes possible for the Divine Spirit to recreate us and make us anew in His own image. In the Silence, we have no desire to exercise the contrary will and the false imagination, for we acknowledge that these are the cause of all our troubles. In the Silence our one desire is that we should be conformed to the likeness of His Son. Therefore, as we abide in the Silence, God is able to work His own perfect will and design in us, and to make us like unto Himself. To quote Jacob Boehme again:

"Blessed art Thou therefore if Thou canst stand still from self-thinking and self-willing, and canst stop the will of the imagination and senses; forasmuch as hereby Thou mayest arrive at length to see the great Salvation of God, being made capable of all manner of divine sensations and heavenly communications. Since it is naught but thine own hearing and willing that do hinder thee, so that Thou dost not see and hear God".

Proceeding, we take the next part of verse three:

He leadeth me in the Paths of righteousness, for His name's sake.

The Lord leads us in paths of righteousness. If we follow the Lord, then we are led in the right path. We all need to do the right thing at the right time, so that harmony ensues. Through following the Lord our actions are right and true. Right action leads to order. Righteousness means following the Lord and doing the will of God in all things. The only result of this can be Divine order, for where the Divine will is done in love, there is Heaven. We do not need to wait until the afterlife in order to find Heaven, for we can establish Heaven now, just where we are, by following the Lord, and doing the will of Heaven, now.

The Lord always leads in Paths of Righteousness those who follow Him. This is so, because the one who is perfect can travel only along paths of order and perfection. If we do not follow Him, then we find ourselves in positions of disorder; for we cannot of ourselves be righteous, neither can we find the right path, because we have not the wisdom that is necessary. When, however, we follow the Lord, we follow the One who is Infinite Wisdom, Intelligence, Knowledge, and Understanding, therefore we are led in Wisdom's way, in a perfect way, in the only way that is perfect, and so a state of Divine order or rightness, or righteousness is brought about.

The Restoring Value of the Silence

This, of course, applies to all exterior action, but it applies still more to finding God in the Secret Place, when we can rest in a state of awareness and realisation of Truth.

If our life is in a state of disorder, and if we are disorderly in our thoughts, habits and conduct, then, resting in the Secret Place and contemplating the Divine, will bring order into our life by changing us into a state of order. The Lord leads us in Paths of Righteousness, or into a state of order, through conforming us to His own likeness, as we wait quietly upon Him, abiding in His presence, acknowledging that of ourselves we can do no good, but that all good comes from God, the Supreme Good, and Source of all Good.

We can never go wrong with affirmative prayer if we base it on the model of the Twenty-third Psalm, for the reason that it puts the Lord first the whole time. The Lord is my Shepherd. The Lord maketh me to lie down in green pastures. The Lord leads me beside the waters of quietness. The Lord restoreth my soul. The Lord leads me in the paths of righteousness. If we always put the Lord first in this way we put self in the background, thus making it possible for God to become all in all, so that there is no false self or ego left. The more we meditate upon Truth, and declare it, and the more we contemplate the Divine, the more completely new our life becomes, and we ourselves also. Indeed, it is a new self that arises. But this is a great mystery, and it is contained in the words of St. Paul: "The first man is of the earth, earthy; the second man is the Lord from Heaven". The Lord or Man of Heaven is born in us from above. No man hath seen God at any time. Man cannot of himself rise up to God, but God has to stoop down in order to raise man up. "He became man, that we might be made God", to quote the words of St. Athanase. Meaning, by this that God comes and dwells in us by His Spirit and changes us into His own likeness; and this life of God in us, or Christ in us, becomes all in all, and our real Self. It is the Divine Spirit dwelling in us that changes us and brings to us the Eternal Life which we ourselves do not possess, apart from God. As in Adam all die, so in Christ all are made alive. The Adam man has to die, in order that Christ may live in us and be all in all. I die daily, said St. Paul. Through putting the Lord first always, the old nature dies, and as it dies, the Divine Spirit takes possession so that we become a new creation.

The Path of Life

The Twenty-third Psalm is helpful in many ways. If used, it will calm the mind and bring us into a state of knowing and awareness, in which wonderful things become possible. But it does more than this; it shows us the path of life, how to travel it, and how to reach our journey's end, the soul's goal, which is the dream of the ages come true. All that has ever happened in the Universe has been but a prelude to this great event, the greatest thing in Heaven and earth. Indeed, the whole object of Creation, world upon world, universe upon universe, is to lead up to this greatest of all events, the changing of man into Man.

In our consideration of the Twenty-third Psalm, we have completed the first of the three stages of our journey. This is one of uneventful harmony, overcoming and blessing. The next stage is of a much more eventful and difficult character; but, because of this, much more worthwhile. The first stage of the new life is cloudless, and it's full of sunshine and joy. So lovely and peaceful is it, and so blessed, that we rationally think that we have already attained. Sin, temptation, habit, weakness, and all the troubles and trials of life seem far away, and we feel quite sure that the old life is dead, and also the old self and that all will be plain sailing forevermore.

But we have not attained fully; we have attained certainly to a point, but it is only a preparation for what is really the most important stage of our journey - the middle stage. It is the most important stage because it is at this point that many break down. Some break down because they have not sufficient staying power; others because they do not realise, or will not acknowledge, that it is necessary to pass through a time of test and trial of strength and endurance, in order that their suitability for the high office to which God is calling them may be demonstrated.

A Divinely Natural Process

As we shall see when we come to examine the fourth verse, there is nothing of which to be afraid. The Lord is guiding us all the time, and everything that takes place is for our highest good.

It is helpful if we understand, with regard to our soul's unfoldment, that it is a natural process; Divinely natural, if you will, but natural, nevertheless. Regeneration is as Divinely natural as generation is physically natural. First, conception, the growth in the dark, and finally emergence into the world, as a completely separate individual. It is as natural as the changes which lead up to the butterfly. First, the grub, eating its way through life, and knowing nothing better. Next comes the chrysalis stage of darkness, during which it seems that no progress is made, but actually, of course, the most amazing changes take place. Lastly, the emergence into the sunlight of a beautiful creature with wings, and ability to fly.

When we realise that the three stages of the life of soul-unfoldment are as natural as the ones just described, we regard the experience of the middle stage differently. I cannot describe it, but the whole life seems different, when we realise that we are merely passing through experiences which if met in the right way are preparation for, and a stepping stone to, our final attainment.

CHAPTER FOUR

I Will Fear No Evil

Let us now proceed to examine the fourth verse. Up till now we have been dealing with the first stage of the Life of Liberation, which means the course or way of life which leads finally to Liberation. The object of life is that we should find Life; that man should become Man, by discovering the Word in his own soul; and this is achieved through the Life of God in the soul. Concurrently with this growth of God-life within the soul, the outward man passes through experiences which gradually change him until he ceases to be an earth man, becoming a Heavenly Man instead.

> The first man is a man of earth, earthy; the second man is from Heaven.
>
> Corinthians 15:46-48

The Heavenly man is born in us from above. "There is one supreme fact of life which is so largely left out of account, because man generally has not awakened to it. It is the fact of the life of God in the soul. It is that real life in man, which expressing is as light shining through darkness" [Richard Whitwell].

A caterpillar could never attain to the butterfly stage if there were not hidden within it the potential butterfly. In the same way, we cannot become anything of ourselves, but the Heavenly man in us may become gloriously manifest. Just as the caterpillar has to cease existence as a caterpillar, and be entirely changed, through a new and better idea becoming manifest, so that it becomes a new creature; so also do we, as the old Adam, cease to be, while in its place grows up the Man from Heaven, who becomes our Real Self.

The Same Individual

Also, just as in the case of the caterpillar which remains the same "individual", in spite of the fact that it becomes changed into an entirely new creature; so also in our case, although we become an entirely new creation, we still remain the same individual.

Imagine, for the sake of illustration, that we possessed a pet caterpillar, and that we called him Sammy. When he reached the butterfly stage, he would still be Sammy, and we should still call him by that name; and, although so greatly changed, outwardly, he would still be the same individual that we knew when in the grub stage. Although Sammy is so low down in the scale of life, we yet realise that he has an individuality all his own, and it is that which we call Sammy. It is the same individual that we recognise in the butterfly; and so we still call him Sammy. Please forgive this kindergarten like illustration, but I want to make this perfectly clear, because there seems to be some misunderstanding on the matter. Some people seem to be afraid that when they attain to Divine union, they will lose their identity. This is a false alarm, for they will never have to do this; but there is a time in our experience when we may have to be willing to give up even our personal consciousness. At such a time, however, we are not only willing, but we actually want to do so; and when we "lose our life" in this way we really find it; for we leave behind the restricted life of the man of separation, and then find that we have found the larger life of God.

The Entering of the Spirit

At one time I was not able to appreciate beauty either in Nature or in Art. The beauties of Nature were not revealed to me because I was not yet capable of appreciating them. In the same way, a picture failed to reveal anything to me, because I lacked something spiritual in my makeup. But a time came when Nature revealed her beauties to me, and pictures also were able to convey to me something of that which was in the mind and soul of the artist when he painted them. Yet Nature was the same, and so were the pictures. The only change that had taken place was in my own soul. What had happened was that the Spirit of Beauty had entered into my soul. Because the Spirit of Beauty had entered my soul, I was able to see beauty everywhere. I was the same individual, yet I was completely changed, because of the Spirit of Beauty living in me. Thus was I saved from my wilderness state of inappreciation of beauty. The Spirit of Beauty entering into, and living in, my soul, was my salvation, as far as the appreciation of beauty was concerned.

In the same way, when God enters our soul by His Spirit, and dwells in our soul, He is our salvation, and we see God everywhere.

As in the Natural, so in the Spiritual

I also want to make this analogy between the caterpillar and butterfly changes, and the changes which take place in us, quite clear, because the Twenty-third Psalm sets forth the Heavenly or Celestial counterpart of the natural three-fold existence and change which are peculiar to lepidopterous insects.

The first stage of the Path described in the first three verses is analogous to the grub or caterpillar stage. It is quiet, harmonious, uneventful, and every need is abundantly met. It is a preparation for greater things to come. It is, however, in a sense, an attainment. It is the highest state of attainment which it is possible to reach at this stage.

The next stage corresponds to the chrysalis period, when there may be darkness, and no apparent progress; yet it is a stage of tremendous and wonderful preparation. This is described in the fourth verse.

The last stage is this stage of glorious attainment, and this corresponds to the butterfly stage of the lepidopterous insects. These start life as humble grubs which can simply crawl and eat: they finish up as winged insects so beautiful that they enchant our eyes as they flutter by us in the sunshine.

Here let me quote one of Henry Victor Morgan's poems, which is very apt and fitting at this juncture:

WINGS

A mystic worm, one summer day,
A worm that dreamed mid creeping things,
Was known to stop up on its way
And say, "I wish that I had wings".
Then all the worms that nearby lay
Laughed long and loud - poor silly things! –
And cried, "Put all such dreams away;
You're but a worm - you'll never have wings".
And one grave worm more wise than all,
(Doctor of Worm Philosophy)
Shook his wise head and said, "I call
This talk of wings rank heresy".
But still the dreamer dreamed his dreams;
Whene'er he looked at flying things
He crept more fast, and said, "It seems
I'll fly like that when I have wings"
One day he felt so chill and numb,
His body pierced with deadly stings;
But dreaming still, e'er death was come,
Said, "Surely this will bring me wings".

Today I saw on wings of fire
This occult dreamer of the dust,
And as it circled glad in air
There came to me this living trust:
That every dream and fond desire,
These longings strange for better things,
Are not in vain; sometime, somewhere,
These dreams of ours will end in wings.

If we read grubs instead of worms in the above poem we have a lovely picture of the great mystical truth of regeneration.

In the Twenty-third Psalm a similar change is set forth. At first, we are sheep and nothing more; stupid, prone to wander, liable to get into trouble, and yet satisfied, so long as we can get enough to eat and drink, and a quiet place to rest.

In the fourth verse we are still sheep - and here the analogy is not quite perfect - but in the fifth verse, what a change has come about! However, this will be dealt with later.

But in spite of this tremendous and revolutionary change, we are still the same individual. Sammy is still Sammy, in spite of the fact that he has changed into an entirely new creation.

Now let us examine the fourth verse. It begins with:

Yea, though I walk through the valley of the shadow of death

The Eastern shepherd, when one pasture was exhausted, had to lead his sheep to other pastures. This necessitated the passing through of dark valleys and gorges where death and danger in the form of wild animals lurked behind every rock and clump of bushes. That is why the shepherd always walked in front of the sheep. He did this in order that he might guard the sheep by being the first one to be attacked, and by fighting on their behalf.

> And Moses said unto the people: Fear ye not, stand still, and see the Salvation of the Lord, which He will show you this day. The Lord shall fight for you, and ye shall hold your peace.
>
> Exodus 14: 13-14

It is necessary that we should pass through the dark valley of experience, but, while doing so, the Lord fights for us. Therefore, the Psalmist says:

> I will fear no evil, for Thou art with me.

In the midst of trouble and danger, in darkness and peril, when the light of the sun is cut off, and when the chill wind of adversity moans through the valley, and awful suggestions

come to us, here is our affirmation of power: ***I will fear no
evil.***

I will fear no evil because *Thou* art with me. Not Jehovah but
Thou, is the word used. In the day when all things go well with
us we speak of the blessing of Jehovah, and how it maketh
us truly rich. But, in the day of trial and trouble, we address
ourselves directly to the Lord. We do not speak *of* Him, or
about Him, but *to* Him. Trouble and danger bring us into a
closer contact with God, and into an intimate fellowship with
Him. We learn to know God in a new and personal way and
speak to Him as friend to friend.

> Henceforth, I call you not servants (or slaves):
> but I have called you friends.
>
> John 15:15

I will fear no evil. I will not trouble my poor brain with intellectual arguments about "the problem of evil". It is sufficient
for me to know that because the Lord is with me, no evil
can come nigh me. It is sufficient for me to know that the
Lord, who is infinite might, power and goodness, into whose
presence no evil dare come, is protecting me. It is sufficient for
me to know that evil has power only on its own plane, and that
it cannot enter the pure presence of the Lord.

It is sufficient for me to know that so long as I follow and
obey the Lord, I live in His presence and am kept free from
all evil. Sufficient for me to know that so long as I can live

consciously in the presence of God, for me there can be no evil; but what may appear to be evil circumstances can be only Infinite Wisdom and Love working out a perfect purpose in my life, a purpose which seeks to raise me Heavenwards.

The Lord who goes in front bearing the brunt of the experience, and who fights for me when evil powers threaten to overwhelm my soul, does so because of His great love to me. His love is so great He takes the post of danger and suffering. He does not leave me to my fate, to fall a prey to ravening wolves, but He goes in front, giving himself, in order to protect me.

I am the Good Shepherd, The Good Shepherd giveth his life for the sheep.

The Lord of Heaven and earth gives Himself, His all, for me, and for you, and for all men. This process of giving goes on perpetually. Heaven is constantly stooping down in order to raise man up. It must always be so, because God is love. We cannot raise ourselves. The lower cannot raise itself to the higher, but the Higher can stoop down and raise the lower to its own level, because it possesses both the power and will to do so. If man could raise himself, he would be God instead of man. Man is not God, but he can become an open channel for the inflow and outflow of Divine life and power. He can become so receptive to God, that he becomes filled with God, even as the branch of the Vine is filled with the life and sap of the Vine. The branch is not the Vine itself, but it is in the Vine, and the life of the Vine flows through it, and is its true life.

Not Fighting but Trusting

At this point let us notice that it is not the sheep who fight the lions and bears which lurk in the shadows, but it is the Good Shepherd, and He alone. A sheep would cut a sorry figure trying to fight either a lion or a bear, even if it could raise courage enough to attempt to do so. A sheep would be very foolish to attempt anything of the kind. It is the Good Shepherd who does all the fighting. He has taken upon himself all the dangers and risks of defending the sheep. What the sheep have to do is to keep close to Him, thus allowing Him to protect them. If they try to fight, they are useless; if they wander away, they fall into danger. Their only hope of safety lies in their keeping close to their Shepherd.

It is precisely the same with us. If we try to fight the evils which threaten to overwhelm us, we are miserably defeated. For instance, if we try to overcome an evil habit, by fighting it, it simply becomes stronger. It is the same with everything else. If we resist evil, it becomes greater. We can never overcome sin by fighting it; neither can we escape from it by running away from it.

It is the same with trouble. We can never overcome it by fighting it. Yet, we can never get the better of it by running away from it. It has to be faced and met, yet to fight it is to deliver ourselves into the hands of the enemy.

If Israel had put their faith in their men of valour, their armies and their arms, they would have been defeated. Instead, they wisely allowed the youth David, who was full of the Spirit to meet Goliath, and to defeat him, not by might nor by power, but by the Spirit of Jehovah. This story symbolises the battle of the soul. If we rely upon the arm of flesh, and the chariots and horses of Egypt; or in other words, if *we* fight against the evil that assails us, then we are defeated. But, if we rely on the spirit, then the infinite power of the Infinite One overcomes for us.

Evil is invincible on its own plane, and so long as we meet it on its own plane, we experience defeat. When, however, we take our stand in God and Truth we are raised above the plane upon which evil operates. In the Twenty-third Psalm the Shepherd represents God coming down to our plane and conquering for us. But He conquers for us by raising us up to a higher consciousness, and in so doing we are brought to the third or last stage of our journey.

The tests and trials of life are both difficult and great. They test and try us to the utmost. It seems at times that we can never win through. Indeed, this is the case, if we think that *we* have to overcome, instead of the Spirit. "Not by might nor by power, but my spirit sayeth the Lord of hosts". The more we are defeated and baffled, the more necessary it becomes for us to surrender ourselves to the Supreme Will and Purpose. When we give up self-effort, acknowledging that all our attempts to conquer are in vain, we cast ourselves upon God with such abandon and completeness that the Spirit is able to do that which is impossible to man. It is not then a question of fighting on our part, during our passage through the dark valley, but of trusting the Good Shepherd of our souls, who alone can bring us victoriously through all life's experiences and uphold us in the great crises of life. Paradoxically, while it is true that in one sense we must not fight, yet it is equally true that we must fight all the time; but such fighting is against our natural inclination to trust to the arms of flesh and human might and power, in the time of danger. Also, we have to fight against our inclination, when things go well with us, to become slack and weak, and slothful, and give in to the sleep of death.

We have to be continually on the alert, so that at the first sign of evil thought, or fear, or suggestion, or at the first sign of trouble, we can reverse it all. We do not have to fight "appearances" or negative ills, but to realise the Truth. Taking our stand in God, or trusting the Spirit, or following the Good Shepherd, all mean the same thing, viz., taking our stand in Truth, instead of being intimidated by appearances.

Yea, though I walk through the valley of the shadow of death I will fear no evil for Thou art with me.

This is a complete reversal of human thought. It switches our thought over from the human to the Divine, from appearances to Reality, and from the lie of the tempter to the truth of God.

When we are faced by terrifying experiences, either in our outward life of practical affairs or in the tests and trials of the soul, when all seems lost, how can we switch over from the terror and appearance of evil to the Reality of perfect security, order and peace? By making use of the words of this fourth verse of the Twenty-third Psalm: *"I will fear no evil, for Thou art with me"*

Here is a short, positive, affirmative, ejaculatory prayer which can be used at all times of stress. It refuses to accept evil suggestion but affirms the presence and power of God. It at once brings us back to our Centre where alone are Truth and Reality. After all, the only thing that we need [and really *want*, if we examine ourselves] is Truth, which of course is Reality. Intuitively, we know that if we can only find Truth, and know it, and abide in it, then all our troubles, difficulties, and fears must become things of the past. Of course, we cannot find Truth with the human mind, neither can we grasp or understand it by the use of the intellect. It comes, however, to our soul like the dawn stealing over the earth after a dark night, or like the refreshing dew falling on the parched earth. The strain and effort of striving after an intellectual understanding do but keep Truth away, or rather, they create barriers which prevent it from entering. The Dawn comes without strain; the dew falls without effort. This is the way of the Spirit; always silently, without strain, without effort.

When we declare Eternal Truth; that is, when we use affirmative prayer, we take our stand in Truth and Reality. In other words, we are brought back to our Centre. If we contemplate and dwell upon our difficulties, weaknesses, failures and sins we depart from our Centre. But when we declare the Truth, positively, we return to our Centre.

Keep, therefore within the Centre, and stir not from the Presence of God revealed within Thy soul.

Jacob Boehme

Following and keeping close to the Good Shepherd, means taking our stand in Eternal Truth. It means that we refuse to accept evil suggestion; it means that we refuse to be dominated by appearances; it means that we recognise God alone, and God's perfection, wholeness, and good. If we are threatened by sickness, instead of thinking in terms of illness, depression and gloom, thus allowing the threatened evil to dominate us and tower above us, we take our stand in God, who is infinite life, health, wholeness and joy. If we are threatened by trouble, difficulty, loss, disaster, we refuse to recognise it, and instead recognise only God and God's presence, in which there is only order, harmony, beauty and all possible good.

If we are threatened by fears for our soul, then, instead of listening to the tempter, we take our stand in God, affirming and realising that He is our Father, that we are eternally loved and cared for, and that we are rooted in That which changeth not, and that our life is lived in God, and His life is in us.

When we are in trouble, or when danger threatens, we may not find it easy to take our stand in God, or to keep our mind stayed upon God. Whatever is troubling us or assaulting us keeps on dragging us down. We may think that we could get on quite well if we had no trouble to try us, and no danger to affright us; but actually, trouble and danger are the very things which enable us to establish ourselves in God and Truth. Again and again, we find ourselves back on the old level with our troubles towering above us. But again and again we turn to the Lord and become raised in consciousness above our troubles and the plane of evil, to the Divine plane of liberty, perfection, order and wholeness.

The Lord Fights Evil: We Fight Ourselves

Life is indeed a battle, but it is not a battle against evil, but against ourselves and our proneness to fall down into the lower consciousness, endeavouring to meet the evil and trouble on its own plane. The great struggle is not with the temptations or suggestions of the evil one, but with our inclination to trust in the arm of flesh instead of becoming allied with the Living God, and united with Him through the Christ consciousness.

I am repeating and emphasising this point, because of its great importance. It is important because it is the secret of overcoming. It is the only way whereby we can be truly positive; by which we can live successfully the life of faith: become victorious in all the experiences of life and be upheld in the great crises of life.

No matter how much we may slip down in consciousness, nor how often we may do so, we must keep on rising again in consciousness, persevering and persisting until we enter into a state of awareness and realisation.

This is the object of the Psalms, to raise our consciousness to the Divine consciousness of Power, Understanding, Wisdom, Perfection, Order and Love; to that level of God-knowing, in which the impossible becomes possible, and all things are accomplished without effort. And this is how the Psalms help us; that is, if we make use of them. They awaken within us an inward spiritual faculty of direct knowing from the standpoint of Universal Truth. They bring into action the dormant Spiritual Mind which can understand the spiritual truths which are foolishness to the ordinary mind and human intellect, and yet are the deep mysteries of God.

The essential thing, then, is that we discover this inner secret which has been hid from before the foundations of the world. This liberating truth or understanding has always been present, but hidden, secret or latent. No one is prevented from entering into Truth, but each one has to find his own way. In his search, however, he is helped by the Spirit. Also, if he perseveres, he is sure to find the object of his seeking; for "he that seeketh findeth".

The Psalms, or rather, some of them, are a great help. They are a help because their object is to raise the consciousness into a state of realisation, in which the power of material things cannot touch us, and also in which the instantaneous, silent, effortless action of God takes place. For, as someone has said, we do not have to fight; we do not have to struggle; we have only to know Truth or God.

Every difficult experience in life becomes either a blessing or a curse, according to the way we meet it. If, through it, we seek and find God, hiding ourselves in Truth, then it becomes a stepping stone to higher things. If, however, we fight and struggle with it on its own plane, it becomes a slippery place down which we slide to disaster.

The Greatest of All Experiences

It is during this stage described in the fourth verse, which some people term Redemptive Tribulation, that the greatest of all experiences come to us. It is at this time that the death of the self takes place. In it we are brought to the end of our tether. The nature of the experiences varies with the individual, but the effect is the same. With some it may be a sin which persists in spite of all efforts and prayers, until the cry is wrung from the heart as it was from St. Paul, "For the good that I would I do not: but the evil which I would not, that I do.... O wretched man that I am! Who shall deliver me from the body of this death?" Or it may be some other form of trouble, like St. Paul's thorn in the flesh, which even prayer could not remove. Or, again, it may be that the experience is similar to that of the mother of the young man who later became St. Augustine. The young man was dissolute, and the more his mother prayed, the more dissipated he seemed to become. There was continual prayer, but for years there was no answer.

Or the experience may be something quite different from any of these that I have described. It may be soul darkness, and apparently the total loss of God's presence. But they're all alike in one respect, they all bring us to a point of failure and despair. It is when we admit our utter and complete failure, impotence and worthlessness, and when we cast ourselves into the abyss of nothingness, giving up our self, our all, and even our life and consciousness of existence, it is then that we find ourselves firmly held in the clasp of God's hand, and are upheld in the Everlasting Arms.

It is through this terrific experience that we find God and also, incidentally, find our true selves. It is after this change, that we know, where formerly we have only believed. It is after this transformation that we know ourselves to be rooted and grounded in the Eternal, and in a state of living union with That which changeth not. It is then that we feel within us the Eternal Word, and the Power of the Infinite thrilling us.

Jakob Boehme (or one of his commentators) says somewhere that we cannot know Truth if we do not *feel* it. This is perfectly true. When we have passed this, the greatest of all experiences that can come to us, we become filled with a Power that thrills us.

When the great change has taken place, we are ready to emerge from the dark valley into the Light and glory of the last stage of unfoldment.

But we are not the same, any more than the butterfly is like the grub which it once was. The psalm describes us as sheep during the first two stages; but in the last stage we are no longer sheep, but... however, this final part of the psalm must be left over to our next chapter.

In closing this instalment may I say a word or two about the last sentence of verse four.

Thy rod and Thy staff they comfort me.

The "rod" used by the shepherd was a sort of light club, sometimes covered with spikes, with which he fought the wild beasts which attacked the sheep. Mention of the rod therefore symbolises the Lord fighting for us in deadly combat with that which otherwise would quickly destroy us.

The "staff" was the shepherd's crook with which he rescued those sheep which wandered away and fell into holes and crevices from which they could not extricate themselves. This symbolises God's saving grace. By His love he rescues and saves us in spite of ourselves, and in spite of our foolishness, our wanderings and our waywardness. Who is there amongst us who cannot testify to the saving grace and loving restoration that he has received at God's hands?

These two things, say the Psalmist, "comfort" him. By "comfort" is not meant sentimental soothing, but being filled with new courage, confidence and strength. Instead of weakening us, as a soothing "dope" would do, it fills us with new life and power. The fact that the Lord fights for us, and also rescues us, even when we wander, gives us confidence and strength, because we know that if we will only perform our part by doing our best to follow Him then we will surely be brought victoriously through all the experiences of the Dark Valley, even into a state of union with the Divine.

Chapter Five

The Dream of the Ages

Blessing Upon Blessing

We have now arrived at the third stage of the Path of Liberation, as set forth in the Twenty-third Psalm; and we notice that a great transformation has taken place. In the first stage the Psalmist speaks of himself as a sheep. In the second stage he still likens himself to a sheep, but a sheep in danger and darkness, through which, however, he is brought victoriously by the Great Shepherd of souls. But in the third stage he is no longer a sheep. A sheep does not have a banqueting table prepared for it, neither does it have its head anointed with oil, nor a cup or chalice given it.

In this third stage we find ourselves not sheep, but princes of the Royal House. No longer are we animals of the earth with our eyes cast downwards, always searching for earthly things with which to satisfy our earthly appetite. Instead, we find ourselves to be miniature replicas of God [like dewdrops reflecting the sun], sons and daughters of the Most High, with our body erect, and our face turned upwards towards the stars.

The Dream of the Ages

The Dream of the Ages has come true; the Divine Purpose in man has reached its fulfilment; the greatest thing in heaven and earth has been achieved: man has left the shadow and found the Substance; he has discovered his true life in God.

> God standeth in the congregation of the mighty;
> he judges among the gods...
> I have said, ye are gods, and all of you are children
> of the Most High.
>
> Psalm 80: 1 and 6

Yet, as Saint Augustine says, "He called men gods, as deified by his grace, and not born of His substance". Therefore, we acknowledge that we owe everything to Divine Grace, and that the change that has been wrought in us has been entirely the work of the Spirit.

Having passed through the Valley of the Shadow, or the period of Redemptive Tribulation, during which everything that would hinder us [that is, everything the self loves], and which would prevent us from entering into the Kingdom of conscious sons and daughters of God, has been removed from us [or surrendered], including the last shred of pride, we find ourselves in a state of Divine union. The soul is now united with its Lord, and the consciousness expanded, so that we see God everywhere, and also feel and know that we are established in the Eternal, and that there is no place but the Here and no time but the Now.

Duties Remain

But the material life continues, the life of the senses continues, and duties have to be performed, and obligations met; but everything is different, for life is transformed by Divine Love.

Actually, we are at the beginning of a new life, a new creation. The old life is dead, but progress still continues, and we pass from victory to victory, and go from strength to strength, and are drawn by the Spirit, ever upwards, to higher and better and more glorious things.

The old life is dead. The old evils and terrors and habits and sins, and devils which afflicted us have all been killed, not by our arm of flesh, but by the Good Shepherd Who fought for us in the dark valley. In the remainder of the Psalm there is no more mention of evil. The last portion describes the state of blessedness as great as that in the first portion, but of a more wonderful and exalted kind.

An Impressive Correspondence

With all reverence may I suggest that the three stages set forth in the Twenty-third Psalm find their counterpart, or correspondence, in the ministry of Jesus. The first stage was one of healing, teaching, and blessing. In spite of the deadly hatred of the orthodox religious leaders of that day, this stage can be called one of harmony and also success, for He was protected by angelic powers, performed many great works, and was successful in all His wordy bouts with his accusers. After this came the inevitable middle stage of darkness. Gethsemane, with its surrender and acceptance of the cross, the giving up of his angelic protection, so that the orthodox religious leaders might insult, scourge and torment Him, and then brutally kill Him.

There is, however, a great difference between the way David's version of the Shepherd of men overcomes for us in the dark valley and the way that the Lord Jesus overcame for us. The Shepherd of the Twenty-third Psalm fights for us; but the Lord Jesus [the Word made flesh], overcame by non-resistance, by submission, and by surrender. It was through these that our Lord's third stage of resurrection and glory was made possible.

After this came the reappearance of our Lord in his glorified body, which was like his earth body, but of Eternal Substance.

We, in a very small way, are called to follow Jesus; but instead of a physical death we have to pass through a mystical death, in which the self is surrendered, so that Christ can reign in our hearts and become our All in All. In this great surrender we lose the false life and consciousness which have kept us from Divine Union, only to discover in their place our true life lived in God and the higher consciousness in which we see God everywhere and all events in the light of Eternity.

Living in the Eternal

The conscious child of God knows himself to belong to Eternity; and he lives his life as an eternal being. He is lifted above the material consciousness into that Presence or Higher Consciousness in which there are no problems or limitations at all, but only order, beauty and perfection, harmony, wholeness and completeness.

Whereas in the old consciousness everything seemed above him, his troubles on top of him, and what he wanted far away; now he looks down on life and its difficulties and finds himself expressing the very things which he at one time longed for, but which seemed beyond his reach.

To live in this state of conscious unity with the Higher and Complete, the Real and Eternal, is to live a life of victory. It means being poised and serene, balanced between or above all conflicting forces. It means living one's life in a state of effortless balance, like the stars and planets, which are poised in space, pursuing their respective courses with effortless precision.

The Twenty-third Psalm has its counterpart also in the parable of the Prodigal Son. First, his life with his father - a son, yet in a state of innocence that is due to inexperience and lack of knowledge. Next comes his journey into time and space conditions, in which he dwells midst "pairs of opposites" conditions during which he learns to appreciate good, through experience with evil. Lastly, there is his return to his Father's house, made wiser by experience, where he receives a royal welcome. Nothing is too good to give to the returned son; no honour is too great to shower upon him.

A similar condition of things is described in the fifth verse of the Twenty-third Psalm. No blessing is too rich, no honour too great, to bestow upon the attained soul.

Thou preparest a table before me in the presence of mine enemies

God does nothing by halves; there is no meanness or stint where He is concerned. He does not give us a crust on the doorstep, but He seats us at the banqueting table, which He has prepared specially for us.

After all that we have been through, and because of our many sins, wanderings, back-slidings and shortcomings, we feel very humble; and like the Prodigal son we would be content with servant's fare in some forgotten corner. But the Lord will have none of this. Although we would fain take the very humblest and meanest seat, He refuses to let us remain here, but says, "Friend, go up higher" Then our Lord proceeds to heap upon us every possible blessing and favour.

In the Presence of the Thing We Once Feared Most

And all this is done in the presence of our enemies. But they all have to keep their distance now, for they no longer have any power to touch or hurt us. Even our greatest enemies, our negative thoughts, doubts and fears - which, all too long, dishonoured God - no longer have any power over us. The Lord has conquered them all and has delivered us from their dominion and from the powers of darkness which sought to devour our soul, by raising us up to His own level, and causing us by His grace to live in heavenly places, where evil can find no entrance and therefore possesses no power over us.

Our enemies, like a pack of snarling, disappointed wolves, although they cannot reach us, are a perpetual reminder to us of the fate that would await us, if through spiritual pride, we were to fall, like Lucifer, from grace. Also, they remind us of that from which we have escaped; and how great has been the mercy and love of the Lord towards us, and how wonderful His salvation.

> For Thou has delivered my soul from death, mine
> eyes from tears, and my feet from falling.
>
> Psalm 116:8

But the Psalmist goes even further, for he says: "Thou anointest my head with oil". This was the greatest honour that could be shown to a guest. Not content with preparing a banquet for us and sitting us at it in full view of our enemies, the Lord bestows upon us the greatest honour: He anoints our head with oil. But this act may have even a deeper significance than that of being made an honoured guest. In the Revelation of St. John the Divine we read that the Lord makes us Kings and priests unto God". May not, then, this anointing with oil be a symbol of this great event, for the Kings and High Priests always had their heads anointed to show that they were chosen of God for their lofty office.

The Enriching Effects of Joy and Praise

But anointing our head with oil is not only a symbol of blessing and honour, it is also a symbol of joy. In Isaiah [sixty-first chapter] it speaks of the Lord giving beauty in place of ashes, the oil of joy to take the place of mourning, and a garment of praise for the spirit of heaviness. In these few words are enshrined ideas of the greatest wisdom and a most practical psychology. If we give way to mourning, sadness and depression then we lay ourselves open to negative ills of various kinds. This is why troubles never come singly. The first blow, if allowed to make us depressed, lays us open to further blows of adversity, and so a downward path is taken - down, down, down.

But God would have us exchange our mourning for joy, and depression for praise, so that our negative moods are overcome. Through this change in us the negative ills, which would otherwise afflict us, such as disease, sickness, loss and other forms of disharmony, are kept at a distance. Like the table which the Lord prepares for us in the presence of our enemies, so also does the Lord anoint us in the presence of our enemies. They cannot come nigh us because we are anointed with the oil of gladness, which raises us up above the plane upon which negative ills function. We now are able to see that much of the trouble which we encountered during our Dark Valley period was due to the fact that we allowed our moods to overcome us instead of our overcoming them by the exercise of praise and thanksgiving.

> Rejoice in the Lord always:
> and again I say rejoice.
>
> Philippians 4:4-8

If we had rejoiced more, and mourned less, our stay in the Dark Valley would have been shortened. Now we are raised above wilderness and conditions because we are anointed with the oil of gladness and wear the garment of praise.

The last part of the Twenty-third Psalm is one of adoration and praise, thanksgiving and rejoicing in God. The Psalmist simply cannot express all that he would like to express of his feelings of joy, gratefulness, humbleness and adoration. But what he does say is very wonderful. For instance:

My Cup Runneth Over

As if it were not enough that the Lord should prepare a banqueting table for us and anoint our heads with oil - by so doing showering upon us His love and bounty and crowning us with honour - He also overwhelms us by filling our cup to overflowing. It is not a cup of sorrow that is filled to overflowing. That belongs to the Dark Valley period. It is a cup of blessing that the Lord gives, and it is full of joy and heavenly delight.

He does nothing by halves. The cup of blessing of joy and salvation is not only filled but is filled to overflowing.

> "I will take the cup of salvation and call upon the name of the Lord".
>
> Psalm 116

The cup is a cup of salvation. It is a symbol of Divine Life given by the Lord, poured out without stint; that we, drinking of it, might be filled with the life of God.

The soul has to eat and drink and breathe, in a way similar to the eating, drinking and breathing of the physical body. Therefore, a table is prepared, at which our soul may feed upon heavenly food: a cup is given from which we may drink the very life of God. Also, with our spiritual lungs "we breathe the finer aethers of the breath of God".

Therefore, while we continue to live an outward life, eating of material food, drinking of ordinary water, and breathing the earthly atmosphere, yet we also live inwardly a hidden life and build up a celestial body. This all takes place automatically, as we stay our mind upon God, and make our will one with the Will of God.

God's Promises Apply to Us

As we meditate upon the words of the fifth verse, we realise their truth. We realise that they are not only true about God and about man, the child of God, but they are true of us, personally. This the wonderful thing about the word of God; when we enter into a real understanding of it, we find that it is addressed to ourselves, individually, just as though we were the only being in the universe, apart, of course, from the Supreme Being.

Therefore, as we read and reflect upon the words of the fifth verse, we realise that they are the language of our own soul, when knowing the Truth, it declares it in an affirmative language. And as we realise the truth of the words that we repeat we know that the table prepared for us by the Lord is an Eternal table, that it has always been ready for us, even from before time was. Always has this table been prepared for us, and also the cup overflowing with the Life given. We have no real life of our own, so a cup of life has been eternally prepared for us by the Lord from before the foundation of the world. We realise that we are eternal children of an Eternal God, with all our needs, both spiritual and material, eternally provided for. We realise, even as St. Paul said, that our life is hid with Christ in God, because we are in a state of unity with God. But this is not of ourselves, but is because we have given up ourselves, and have relinquished the self life.

A State of Union

The third stage is one of union with the Divine. Now, Divine Union may still be only a term to some of us; if so it can mean but little to us. But Divine Union in reality [that is, when

we realise it and know it] is the greatest thing to which we
can attain. To be united in consciousness with the perfection
above us is the great secret of all attainment and overcoming.
It is the secret of victory over every sin and weakness, over
sickness and penury, fear and unhappiness. So long as we are
low down in a dark valley of consciousness, then everything is
on top of us, and we are subject to every ill and evil, while the
good that we so much desire seems far beyond our reach.

But, when we become raised up in consciousness, and realise
that we are sons and daughters of God, with every blessing and
good pressed upon us, and that, really and truly, we are one
with all the bounty and blessing and beauty and harmony of
the Heavenly Reality, we find that we are able to express the
very qualities and forms of harmony and good which before
seemed beyond our reach.

Divine union means not only a state of oneness with Divine
purity, and sweetness and goodness of heart, and strength and
nobility of character, but also oneness with the Divine order,
harmony, beauty, wholeness, health and substance.

From this it will be seen that this third stage is a much higher
state of attainment than the first stage, described in verses one,
two and three. The realisation described in those three verses
is like being carried along on a stream of blessedness, and that
from all directions come blessings of every kind. Truly a blessed
experience.

But the third stage is greater far than this. It is the realisation
that we are one with the Source of the Stream of Blessedness

itself. Divine Love brings us into a state of Union with the One Source of all Blessedness, Order, Perfection, Life, Health, Wholeness, Substance and Good.

Having reached this stage we KNOW, where formerly we have only believed. We do not have to seek for Divine good: we do not have to think, even, that it has to come to us; instead, we express it. We carry it with us wherever we go. This is why David said:

> Surely, goodness and mercy shall follow me all
> the days of my life.

Surely - of a surety, with certainty, without a shadow of a doubt - Divine goodness and loving kindness will follow me, always, wherever I go. I do not have to follow them, they follow me. They manifest wherever I may be.

Most of us, I suppose know people of this kind. They carry an infection of health with them. Their atmosphere or presence brings healing to others. Harmony manifests wherever they go, and all restriction and lack disappear at their coming. They express the things of which most people feel the need. They carry with them something which brings about an adjustment, or a restoration, or a correspondence with the One Internal Harmony. Instead of having to run after people and beg their help or cooperation, they "stand in the Eternal ways", after which people come to them of their own volition. And all this is so because they live in the consciousness of Reality.

Hold fast to the Great Idea, and men will come
to you of themselves.

Lao Tsze

This means, holding fast to Absolute Truth in which are included all lesser and relative truths. It means getting to the
Centre and Essence, and staying there; then life becomes complete, and everything that is necessary follows, just as day suc-
ceeds night. It means living in the consciousness that love,
order, perfection, wholeness, beauty and good are the Reality,
recognising that they are the truth, and refusing to acknowledge that any departure from these is true, or has any reality
or substance. God is the only Substance, and we recognise and
acknowledge God only.

Recognizing Divine Order

It also means recognizing God as The One Centre and Cause,
as the Life of our life, without whom we are nothing; and also
that man lives His life in God, and that God's life also is in
him, and that every man, in actual truth and in the Divine
providence, is in his appointed place, at his appointed time,
doing his appointed work, and doing it perfectly. When we
see and realise all this, we have cosmic vision: we are able to
understand the Allness of God, instead of it being merely a
belief with us.

Yes, "hold fast to the Great Idea": the idea of Divine Perfection and order, and we, by Eternal Grace, made part of the Eternal Harmony. God can never fail. His purposes must ever be brought to a victorious completion. His word goeth forth, and it accomplishes its intended task.

> So shall my word be that goeth forth out of my mouth: it shall not return unto me void, but it shall accomplish that which I please, and it shall prosper in the thing where-to I sent it. For you shall go out with joy, and be led forth with peace: the mountains and the hills all break forth before you into singing, and all the trees of the fields shall clap their hands.
>
> Instead of the thorn shall come up the fir tree, and instead of the brier shall come up the myrtle tree: and it shall be to the Lord for a name, for an everlasting sign that shall not be cut off.
>
> Isaiah 55

The Divine order and harmony are ever present; they are the Reality. Let us "hold fast to the Great Idea".

Good Only

It is worthy of notice that David, when describing the third stage of the Path of Attainment makes no mention of evil at all. In the first stage he speaks of the soul having to be restored, owing to it being either weakened or contaminated through contact with evil. In the middle stage the Psalmist refers directly to evil. This is a time when evil makes every effort to destroy us, but the Lord our Shepherd protects us, and defeats it. In the third stage we have been lifted above evil. He can stand afar off and make grimaces at us but cannot approach us. Of a surety, says David, by implication, evil can never touch me again, for goodness and loving kindness shall follow me all the days of my life.

But he realises that he has to remain in the Higher Consciousness if this assertion of his is to remain true in his case, so he adds:

I will dwell in the House of the Lord forever.

David obviously did not mean that he would dwell literally in the House of the Lord, always, but that he would abide in the Presence of the Lord, continually. To the extent that we live in conscious realisation of the Presence of God are we correspondingly maintained in that super consciousness which is above all evil and which knows only order, perfection, and good. God is the Supreme Good, and to live in His presence is to know only good. We think no evil; we speak no evil; we impute no evil; we know only Divine Good, because we live consciously, and in a state of awareness, in the Presence of the Supreme Good.

The Supreme Good, of course, is far above the relative good which we know as distinct from relative evil. Divine Good is a state of order, wholeness, balance and completeness, in which evil disappears, through being brought into its right place. This is termed "being above all pairs of opposites". Those who cannot understand this need not trouble their heads about it. "If any man will do his [God's] will, he shall know of the doctrine", and the problem of evil will disappear as far as he is concerned.

There can be no doubt, I think, that David really did attain to that Higher Consciousness at the time that he wrote the Twenty-third Psalm. He was no doubt guided and inspired by the Spirit when he wrote it, and consequently may not have realised quite the full inner meaning of that which he was led to write; for at such times an inspired writer may write above himself and his present state of attainment and spiritual understanding. The Divine Spirit is thus able to get through something greater than the writer himself is aware of, although he does not write automatically, but consciously. In spite of this I feel sure that David had attained to this higher state of consciousness when he wrote the Twenty-third Psalm. When we read other Psalms of David's it would appear that he did not always live in the high state of consciousness described by him in the 5th and 6th verses. If he had done so then his many failures and sins described in other psalms would never have been possible.

This should be a warning to us all, for the higher we have climbed the greater and more disastrous is our fall, if we do fall, yet climb we must; but the same Lord who brought us victoriously through the Dark Valley "is able to keep us from falling and present us faultless before the presence of His glory with exceeding joy".

To the only wise God our Saviour, be glory and majesty, dominion and power, both now and ever. Amen.

Jude 1:25

Part 2

The Lord's Prayer: A suggested amplification and interpretation for daily use

HAMBLIN
VISION
PUBLISHING

Hamblin Vision Publishing

Preface

The Lord's prayer was never meant for parrot-like repetition. Our Lord said that we should pray "after this manner", that is, that we should base our prayer upon its framework, so to speak.

The following suggested prayer is an amplification and exposition of the Lord's Prayer. By its use the mind becomes stayed upon Divine Truth, so that an understanding and realisation of the great truths enshrined in the Lord's Prayer come to the soul. As a consequence of this the Prayer itself will convey a richer and deeper meaning whenever it is read over, slowly, in its original form as given us in St. Matthew's Gospel or the Prayer Book. The Law of Association will work in such a manner that the deeper understanding will become added to the prayer as it is uttered, slowly and reverently.

What follows should not be read as a book but should be used as a prayerful meditation.

CHAPTER SIX

The Lord's Prayer

AN INTERPRETATION

Our Father Which Art in Heaven

We adore Thee who art the One Centre and Source and Origin of all life, creation and manifestation. Thou art the Beginning and the End, the First and the Last, yet art Thou Thyself without beginning and without end. Thou always hast been, and art and evermore shalt be. Thou art the Causeless Cause; Thou art the Unchanging Reality.

We adore Thee, not only because Thou art Life Itself, and the Origin from which the stream of life continually doth flow, but also because Thou art Love, Joy, Peace, Wholeness, Perfection, Order, Beauty, Harmony and all Good. Yet Thou dost transcend all these attributes and art beyond our highest thought.

We thank Thee and adore Thee, because Thou art our Creator, Preserver and Sustainer. We thank Thee that from Thee cometh our life. We have no life of our own, but all life cometh from Thee, the One Source of life. Therefore, the life that is now flowing through us, is Thy life - the Life which can never decay or grow old.

We reverence and adore Thee. Thou art above every attribute ascribed to Thee. Thou art beyond all our ideas of goodness and perfection. Thou art beyond our highest understanding of love. Thou art far beyond all our conceptions of beauty, order, harmony and perfect rightness. And so we reverence Thee. We adore Thee. We will worship Thy Name forever and ever.

Yet, although Thou art the Light above every light, and the Perfection above every perfection, the Origin and Source of all good, the Power above every power, and so wonderful as to be beyond any words that we can use, yet we are taught to call Thee –

Our Father

Thy Name is above every name - the Name which cannot be uttered. But, although Thy name is too holy and sacred to be uttered [for no name uttered by man could ever describe Thy nature and wondrous perfection], yet we can call Thee - Our Father.

Our Father-Mother God

The Progenitor-Progenitrix. The Source from which we come, and the Haven to which we can return. Oh, how wonderful Thou art! We hide ourselves in Thee.

Our Father which art in Heaven. Thou dost inhabit Eternity. Thou art the Sovereign Lord who art the Light of the Light Realms. Thou art the Order of Heaven, the Harmony of all Harmonies, the Beauty of Holiness, and the Joy of all joys. Thou art the altogether Perfect One, transcending all our thoughts and conceptions of perfection, order, beauty and joy.

Thou inhabitest the Superconscious Realm. Do Thou raise us up to the Superconscious state also; so that our mind may work in unison with Thy Divine Mind, and all our thoughts become Heavenly in character, corresponding to the Divine order and harmony. So, may we know Thy peace and, through grace, be able at all times to abide in it.

Thy Kingdom Come

Let Thy Kingdom of rightness, order, harmony, wholeness, completeness, beauty, perfection and peace come into our heart, our mind, our body, our world, and our life. Let it be made manifest in all our affairs. Especially may Thy Kingdom of order be established in our thought life, in our emotional life, and in our heart, so that our inner life may be conformed to Heavenly standards. May Thy Heavenly Kingdom be firmly and everlastingly established within us, by the casting out of all evil thoughts of envy, resentment, pride, impurity and selfishness, and the implanting within us of Heavenly love, goodwill, humility with firmness, selflessness, and a desire to serve, instead of to make others serve us, to give instead of to get; to pour out ourselves, instead of exploiting others to their detriment and our personal gain.

Thy Will be Done

O Lord of life and Order and Love may Thy will be done. We have no will of our own, except to do Thy will, which is infinitely good, and alone can bring us to our highest good. Experience has taught us that going our own way of self-will leads only to unhappiness and woe. Therefore, "lead Thou me on. I do not ask to see the distant scene. One step enough for me".

We surrender our all to Thee. We give up the contrary will [which has taken us away from Thee], and the false imagination [which has created all the evils of our life], praying that Thy perfect will may take the place of our contrary will, and that Thy perfect imagination may take the place of our false imagination; so that Thy will shall guide us in ways of peace and harmony, and Thy imagination create for us conditions like unto those of Heaven.

In Earth as it is in Heaven

Let Thy will be done in our earthly body, even as it is done in the Celestial body: in our earthly conditions as in the conditions of Heaven: in our earthly life, even as in the life of the Light Realms.

Let Thy will be done in all my vehicles. Let Thy will be done in every cell, atom and particle of my bodily substance. Let Thy will of wholeness reign in every organ of my body, maintaining it in a state of health and perfection.

Let Thy Will be Done in My Mind

Let Thy will direct all my thoughts and make them like unto Thine own. Dissolve every adverse thought, change every mental process that is not God-like, so that my mind and all its workings may be conformed to the Mind of God, which being perfect can think only thoughts that are Divinely and eternally good.

I surrender all my evil habits of thought, and desire only that now and always Thy will should be done in all my thinking, and that all my thoughts should be according to the Mind of Christ.

Let Thy Will be Done in My Affections

May I love only the Good, the Beautiful and the True - that which is pure and lovely and perfect - that which is after Thine own heart.

Let Thy Will be Done in My Actions

May I do all for Thee. May all my actions be Christ-like; may all that I do be an act of service to the world. Let me not work for self but only that others may be blest.

Let Thy Will be Done in My Heart

May I love humanity even as Thou hast loved me. O may I pour out my soul upon all men, even as our Lord "poured out His soul unto death". May my love for humanity be a consuming passion, in which the love of self becomes extinguished forever. Greater love hath no man than this, that he lay down his life [pour out his soul in love so that all love of self dies] for his friends [all humanity].

O Lord of all Life and Love, who has done so much for us, and given so much to us, help us to pour out our soul upon all mankind in blessing and benediction and love.

Dear people, everywhere, I love you all, I love you. May you be Divinely blest, and may you know God's peace, and His love. May every blessing, that I would pray for myself, be yours also; and may you have it abundantly.

Give Us This Day Our Daily Bread

All our supply comes from Thee and from Thee alone. Everything that we need, both for soul and body, has been provided for us from before the foundation of the world. Thou art the One Substance. There is nothing in this world that has any reality or substance of its own. It is only as it is upheld by Thy Substance that it has any substance at all. All things necessary for our life belong to Thee, and Thou alone hast the ordering of them, in spite of appearances to the contrary.

Thou art the Bread of Heaven by which our soul is fed. As we wait upon Thee now, our soul is being nourished and our spirit refreshed. We are feeding upon the Hidden Manna, and finding Thee to be within us as a well of water, springing up into everlasting life.

Now we relax, we breathe deeply according to the Heavenly Rhythm, and interiorly our soul breathes the sweet aethers of the breath of God. Thus, our Inner Man is being nourished, and strengthened, and built up in God-substance.

The silver and the gold are Thine, and the cattle on a thousand hills. Thou art filling us with plenty and crowning our life with loving kindness and tender mercy. All the wealth and substance of the world are nothing in themselves. It is Thy Divine ideas of substance which alone are real and permanent. Therefore, we do not have to lay up treasure on earth, where moth and rust doth corrupt and where thieves breakthrough and steal, but we look to Thee Who art the Source of all true wealth which can never suffer from loss or decay, and which even now is seeking to manifest in abundance in our life, and supply adequately our needs. On Thee, the Unchanging Substance, we rely, and not upon changing, decaying things. Thou dost always manifest abundantly according to our need, as we look to Thee, the Source, instead of to uncertain and frail human and material channels.

And Forgive Us Our Debts As We Forgive Our Debtors

As we forgive others their trespasses towards us, so do we enter into the Divine forgiveness of our trespasses against life and our fellows. Thou, O Father, art all love and forgiveness, but we can enter into them only when we have forgiven our brother his trespasses against us.

At this moment, therefore, we forgive freely all our enemies and slanderers, all who have injured us in any way. We pour out our love and compassion, our forgiveness and mercy upon them, praying that they may be Divinely blest and Divinely prospered, and that they may know Thy peace, and experience all the riches of Thy saving grace.

And Lead Us Not Into Temptation

Lead us, O Father, away from temptation. Thou dost never tempt any man, for man is tempted by his own sinful desires, and not by Thee. Therefore, lead us away from these things. May our vision of Thee be so entrancing that we forget all our desires for sin and selfishness, which, if given attention to, would tempt us away from Thy goodness, purity and perfect order.

Lead us, O Father, in the right Path: may we see only Thy perfection and beauty and loveliness, so that all desire for lower things may die a natural death.

But Deliver Us from Evil

Deliver us, O Father, from the enemy of souls, from all the powers and forces which war against our spiritual life. Protect us from astral invasion, from evil thoughts, from impure suggestions. Thou alone art the Reality: may all these evil things be cast into their native nothingness.

May we know only Thee, Father, the beauty of Thy character, the loveliness of Thy mind, and the perfection of Thy will. May we be so filled with Thy Spirit that there shall be no room for anything unworthy or untrue.

CHAPTER SEVEN

Comments and Notes

The Doxology which generally appears at the end of the Lord's Prayer is not found in the oldest MSS., and, therefore, could not have formed part of the original prayer.

At one point in the above prayer, where surrender is made, the first personal singular is used. This is so personal that it cannot be made in combination with others: it is something which each one has to perform by himself or herself with God alone.

The Lord's prayer is designed to help the personal unfoldment of the one using it. But what about praying for others, it may be asked? If it is a perfect prayer, it should also be capable of being used on behalf of others.

In order to meet this need the following procedure is suggested:

For one's own personal devotion, use the amplified prayer as given in this book, first.

Afterwards, use the Lord's prayer as given in St. Matthew, or the Prayer Book, in the following manner:

First think of your loved ones, gathering them together, in imagination, and putting your arms around them; then repeat the Lord's prayer slowly; at the same time imagining that they are saying it with you.

If you cannot seem to hold one of them, because he or she keeps slipping away from you, pray for that one alone, and keep on persevering and trying to hold him or her up while repeating the prayer. Also, do the same with anyone for whom you wish to pray specially.

Also, for the world at large you can do the same. This will not only help the world, but it will also get rid of egocentricity or self-centeredness, which is the greatest of all hindrances to spiritual progress and unfoldment.

Self-Centredness is Death
Universal Love is Life

Part 3

Bless the Lord, O My Soul: Being some thoughts
suggested by Psalm 103

Hamblin Vision Publishing

Preface

*It is through blessing others that we ourselves be-
come blessed: it is by the blessing of the Lord that
we enter into a state of Divine blessedness.*

Some of us, perhaps, are not aware that complaining shuts
the soul up in a dark dungeon, or that praise and thanksgiving set the soul free. But so it is. St. Paul tells us that one of
the sayings of the Lord Jesus was: "It is more blessed to give
than to receive". Blessing and thanksgiving are a definite act of
giving by the soul. When we bless another, we pour out our
soul upon him, and so he is blessed; but we are greatly blessed
also, because the more we give out, the more fully we become
charged with Divine life and power.

The secret of life is motion, circulation, movement. When
these are impeded, the life force is run low: if they were to
cease, entirely, life would come to an end. There has to be a
continuous circulation, a process of giving and receiving, of
passing on to others whatever we may have to give.

It is owing to this law that the act of blessing and thanks-giving on our part is so beneficial to the soul. Complaining and indulging in self-pity are astringent and stultifying: they withdraw us from the free circulation of life: they confine us in a sort of stagnant backwater, where there can be no freedom, health or joy. Blessing and thanksgiving on the other hand, because they are an act of giving on the part of the soul, bring us out into the free current of life, where are movement, cir-culation, health and joy.

The Psalmist must have known all about this when he called upon all the congregation to say: "Bless the Lord, O my soul, and all that is within me, bless His holy Name". When we do so call upon our soul, we pour out all that we are, and all that we have within, all that constitutes our complex personality, like a flood upon the Name that is above every name. The pent-up waters of life are released, so that the free circulation of life's forces is restored, and we enter into freedom.

Prayer, as popularly understood, is a continual asking. The prayer that sets free is a continuous giving - giving of our soul, giving of all that we have and are, to the Lord in love, blessing and thanksgiving.

> Bless the Lord, O my soul, and all that is within me, bless His Holy Name.
>
> Psalm 103:1

Chapter Eight

Arousing the Soul

Bless the Lord, O my soul: and all that is within me, bless His holy name

The object of the Psalms is to produce an effect upon our mind and soul. Their object is to raise us out of the material consciousness into God-consciousness. Their object is to dismiss from our soul all fear and doubt, to banish from our heart all sadness and gloom, and to establish our mind firmly in Eternal Truth, in which we realise that we are children of Eternity, one with That which changeth not.

There is a reason for this, of course. The Psalmists did not raise the congregations of the people up to these higher states of consciousness, joy, confidence, and faith without having a purpose in view. It was not done in order to make their services "bright and attractive", so that they might have good attendances and collections. The reason why they went about their task systematically to raise their people to a higher consciousness, was in order to help them. It was to protect them when in danger: it was to heal them when they were diseased: it was to make them successful as a nation.

They knew that if they could raise the people to this higher consciousness then no evil could befall them, for they would be surrounded by an atmosphere of spiritual power, against which no evil force of disorder could prevail.

The Psalmists knew that the most effective way to achieve this end was to teach the people to bless and praise the Lord, to tell of His mighty acts, and to call to mind all that the Lord had done for them, in times past, and for his servants in all ages.

> He made known his ways unto Moses: His acts
> unto the children of Israel.
>
> 103rd Psalm, Verse 7

Psalm after psalm begins either with a call to everyone who reads to praise the Lord, or else it starts by actual praise of the Lord. In the 103rd, which is described as a Psalm of David, the poet, in simple, yet magnificent language, calls upon his own soul to bless the Lord.

> Bless the Lord, O my soul: and all that is within
> me, bless his holy name.

These words were given to David for his use, for our use, and for the use of everyone who reads them. They are a call to the deeps within us to bless the Author of our being and the Light of our life. As we proclaim the words with earnestness and fervour, our soul begins to vibrate with the power of the Highest. Ordinarily, our soul is asleep, or in deathlike stupor. Even those of us who have been spiritually awakened, and who have started out on the new life of spiritual attainment, find that our soul falls asleep again, if we do not do something to arouse it. The Psalmist supplies the remedy.

We are to call upon the soul to bless the Lord. When we do so the vibration of the uttered words, which are an expression of the Spirit of God, and therefore powerful, cause sympathetic vibrations to take place in our soul. It begins to arouse itself: it begins to wake up: it begins to become aware of itself, and of its love of God and its need of God.

When we call upon our soul to bless the Lord it is as though we gave our soul a good shaking, saying:

Awake, Thou that sleepest, and arise from the dead, and Christ shall give thee light.

Ephesians 5:14

Through calling upon our soul in this way we bring life to it, so that it becomes thrilled and energised with the vibrations of the Eternal Life of God. By blessing the Lord, our soul becomes "lively", and able to vibrate in harmony with the vibrations of Divine Energy. In other words, new life, Divine Life, comes into our soul, through our calling upon it to praise and magnify God. Thus, the sleepy, almost dead soul, is awakened and made alive, to become-at-one with the one universal Lord or spirit, Who is Life itself, and the One Source of all Life.

Let us note in passing that David, in the 103rd Psalm, does not begin by asking the Lord to bless his soul, but by calling upon his soul to bless the Lord. There is a great difference. There is the difference between the spirit of "getting" and the spirit of giving. Both forms of prayer are necessary, but the prayer of praise, thanksgiving and blessing the Lord is the higher type.

May I point out that God is not a sort of eastern potentate who listens with an ear to our wailings, and then, if we are sufficiently doleful and pitiful, will answer our prayers. God is Universal Spirit, in Whom we live and move and have our being. We are surrounded by the Living Presence of God: call it Mind-Stuff, if you will, but God's Mind-stuff. From this Divine Mind Power or Spirit of Infinite Power, Wisdom, Love and Intelligence, which surrounds us, comes a reaction according to our attitude of mind and soul. According to our attitude the response is either positive or negative. To magnify our wants and weaknesses instead of magnifying the Lord, may increase our wants and weaknesses, instead of reducing them. As explained elsewhere, if we have a great problem or trouble, we have to become free from its dominance and find God and lay hold upon Him. By this is meant entering into the Inner Centre or Central Harmony and Power, and then grasping Truth, by faith. By Inner Centre I mean what the Psalmist meant by the Secret Place of the Most High. This can be illustrated in a simple way. I have used this before, many times, probably, but it is apt and will bear repeating, I think. An electric cable, such as is put underground, is heavily insulated by layers of paper and rubber, both non-conductors of electricity. Such a cable can be handled, and yet no current will be felt, because of the insulated covering which separates us from the metal interior which carries the current If, however, we strip off the covering we can attach wires to the main which will light and heat our house or drive the machinery in our workshop.

In the same way, effective prayer is finding God, or getting to the Centre, and making real contact. The "insulation" which separates us from our Centre is not merely "sin", but the pressure of circumstances, selfishness, self-will, worry, fear, care, anxiety, and so on. We have to get away from all these things, and this we can do, not by magnifying them, or dwelling upon them, but by magnifying the Lord.

The Secret of Blessing

If we want order to manifest in our life, we must first have order in our soul. If we want our soul to be healthy and lively, we must call upon it to bless the Lord, its Divine Source.

David was a practical mystic. He was well aware that a state of order in the outward life depended upon a state of order in the soul life. He knew that if the soul of the people would praise the Lord and rejoice in Him, and if they would walk in His statutes, then they would be blessed; they would be strong, physically, and free from disease; and they would be protected from harm and danger and prospered in all their ways [See Psalm 1.]

The 103rd Psalm is one of great blessings. It enumerates all the most wonderful blessings that can come to man. But there is always a condition that has to be fulfilled. The condition in this case is given in the first verse. If this is fulfilled, then all the wonderful blessings described in the succeeding verses become true of us, but not otherwise.

> Bless the Lord, O my soul, And all that is within me Bless His holy name.

In this verse is contained the secret of a blessed, successful and abundant life. It is the antidote of depression.

Now, depression is the cause of countless evils. It tends to produce disease, sickness, ill health, poverty, and other woes and troubles. It also leaves us open to accidents, disasters, violence, discord and disaster. It takes from us all power to achieve, overcome and make a true success of life.

A depressed soul cuts itself off from God, its one source of life and power. A depressed soul attracts conditions as negative as itself. A depressed soul lays itself open to the forces and powers of disaster and disorder, for it possesses no defence, through not being established in God.

The importance of overcoming depression

David, the poet and singer, knew this: and so did David the man of war, faced by the stark realities of an appallingly difficult life. He knew that if he allowed his soul to be depressed and lifeless, then he himself would fail, and become submerged by the difficulties and dangers which met him and challenged him on every hand. David knew that his only hope lay in galvanising his soul into life and activity, that it might ascend the hills of God, and walk and talk with God. He knew that if he could only achieve this, then everything else would become Divinely adjusted. This was essential, the fundamental and all important requirement. If he could meet it, all would be well. If he did not, then he would be submerged and overwhelmed.

And so David cries to his soul to bless the Lord, and all that is within him to bless His holy name; and by so doing he took the first step towards God-consciousness, which meant health and strength, and success and achievement and overcoming and victory.

What was true of David, in his day, is equally true of us, in our day. If we allow our soul to become depressed, asleep, or torpid, then we make ourselves receptive to every ill to which the flesh is heir, and also lay ourselves open to every form of disaster and disorder. Unless we know better than to do so, we make matters far worse by worrying over the disorderly conditions which we have attracted, instead of turning to the Lord and making our soul to praise Him.

The way to overcome difficult conditions is to overcome the mood of the soul

In Psalm 42 David speaks of being overwhelmed by waves and billows. His way of overcoming was to chide his soul and to call upon it to hope in God. "Why art Thou cast down, O my soul? And why art Thou disquieted within me? Hope Thou in God: for I shall yet praise Him for the help of His countenance".

David recognised that what he had to deal with was not so much his troubles as the condition of his soul. The whole 42nd Psalm is a series of arguments with his soul, in an endeavour to get it back to a state of serenity and joy and peaceful union with God.

In the same way, we can overcome our difficulties only by treating the soul. Within ourselves is the cause of outward disharmonies; therefore, it is only by a change within that healing and restoration can come. If things are going wrong with us externally, then it is the soul that we must treat.

If we want to be master of our life, we must be captain of our soul. We must not let the mood of our soul destroy our happiness, our health, and our work in life. We must call upon our soul to bless the Lord.

If we are a victim of sin, then let us call upon our soul to praise the Lord, because He is the Deliverer from sin. If we are weak, then that our soul praise the Lord for His strength which renews us inwardly. If we are poor, then let our soul praise the Lord for all His riches in glory, and because He desires to bestow upon us every possible blessing and good.

On top of life

Praising the Lord is the way of victory and overcoming. If we do this, then we are always on top of life, instead of submerged by it. If we allow our soul to become discouraged and depressed, then life's difficulties overwhelm us, rearing themselves above us like mountains above the plain. If, however, we call upon our soul to bless the Lord, then we are raised up above life's difficulties, so that we look down upon them, as very little things, and thus are in a victorious attitude; for we realise that "all the Divine forces are hastening to minister to us". But the Psalmist goes farther than just calling upon his soul to bless the Lord, for he adds:

And all that is within me, bless His Holy Name.

All that is within me: heart, mind, affections, character, all that makes up the complete, yet complex "man", all to bless the Lord's holy name.

It is not sufficient that I should write about this verse, and that you should read it. It is necessary that each one of us should utter it, speak it, and give voice to it; for there is power in the spoken word.

Each positive word represents a positive idea. Each word possesses a vibration of its own, so that when uttered it produces an effect like unto its own character. If it is a positive word of Truth it produces in the soul a vibration, or liveliness, like unto itself. We must, therefore not merely read about these things, but must give utterance to the words, which, because they represent Divine ideas, are pregnant with Celestial power. How careful then should we be as to the nature of the ideas upon which we dwell, the thoughts which we think, and the words which we speak.

The first verse teaches us not only to call upon our soul to bless the Lord, but also "All that is within me bless His holy name". We must not hold anything back but surrender all that we have and are to the Lord, dedicating every particle of will, all our affections, our intellect, our powers to the act of blessing the holy name of the Lord.

Not being a scholar, I do not know the meaning of the Hebrew word that has been translated "holy". It may simply mean "sacred", or "hallowed". The English word "holy", however, has other meanings, which are very suggestive. The word "holy" means also, whole, hale, entire, complete. We read in the New Testament of people being made whole through Divine healing. The word "whole", when meditated upon, reveals itself to us as the expression of a lovely idea of perfection, such as is beyond any human attempts at description. We call upon all that is within us to bless the holy name of the Lord of Wholeness. When we do this our soul is made whole or is restored. [See Psalm 23, 3.]

Every particle and atom

But it is not merely that our soul is made whole, but also our body. It is helpful if we make the meaning of "all that is within us" to include all that is within our physical body, meaning by this, all its constituent parts. I find it helpful, personally, to call upon every particle, atom, cell, corpuscle, tissue, vein, artery, organ, within my body, to bless the name of the Lord. This may strike the average reader as being silly and fantastic, but it is not so, for, on the contrary, it is practical and effective. Every part of the body is intelligent and can obey orders. When every particle of the body turns to the Lord, then every particle begins to function properly, according to the Divine plan.

There is a great deal in this idea of calling upon everything to bless the Lord. If we call upon all peoples, and all creatures, and all creation to join with us in praising the Lord of Life, our consciousness expands, so that finally we enter into Cosmic or Universal Consciousness, the goal of every true seeker.

We can join the birds in their grand chorus at daybreak; we can also join in with their evensong. We can sense the silent music of the flowers and join them in their hymnody of praise. In fact, we can call upon everything, of which we have knowledge, to bless the holy name of the Lord. There are special hymnodies and canticles designed for this very purpose, through the use of which the aspirant enters into universal consciousness. Therefore, it is in harmony with the highest mystical tradition to call upon the constituent parts of our body to join with us and our soul to bless the holy name of the Lord of all life, love and power, wisdom, intelligence and understanding. "Bless the Lord, O my soul; and all that is within me, bless His holy name". In the second verse the Psalmist repeats himself, but with an addition. He says:

> Bless the Lord, O my soul, and forget not all His benefits.

In this wonderfully helpful Psalm, we are exhorted, not to ask for benefits, but to remember the Lord's benefits - His love and mercy towards us. The rest of the Psalm is devoted to a description of the benefits of the Lord. The Psalmist's object was not to curry favour with a vain, praise-loving God, but to produce a change of mind and soul on the part of those who would use the Psalm. God does not have to be placated or cajoled. He is unchanging love, wisdom, intelligence, power. He radiates good and blessing like a lighthouse radiating light over the sea. All that is needed is that we should become attuned to the will of God, and the mind and soul raised to higher levels so that they work in unison with the Mind of God, and the One Soul of the Universe. The object of all true prayer, and the use of psalms and canticles, and hymns is simply to bring the soul into a state of union with the Lord, and the mind in a state of oneness with the Mind of God. The 103rd Psalm provides us with the ideal means of becoming at-oned with God. It begins by telling us to call upon our soul to bless the Lord, and then goes on to tell of all His love and mercy, and His wonderful works to the children of men.

If we forget the benefits of the Lord, if we are unmindful of His love, if we return not to render thanks for the innumerable blessings which we have received at His hands [like the nine lepers who never even thanked our Lord for His healing] then we shut ourselves off from God, and thus cut ourselves off from Divine blessing.

But, if we bless the Lord and remember and recite His wonderful blessing and goodness to us, we are raised nearer to God and made receptive to yet more good.

How often are we tempted to complain that our prayers are not answered; yet it is simply due to the fact that we take all our blessings for granted, never give real thanks for them, never bless and praise the Lord, but simply pray and beg for more favours. By so doing, we cut ourselves off from the eternal flow of blessing and good which proceeds from the One Central Fount of love, wisdom, joy and power.

Joy is related to every form of good and blessing

Another reason of our lack of success may well be that we are not joyful. Joy brings us into correspondence and co-relation with all possible good. We may be tempted to say that we will be joyful when we are healed, or when our business or family troubles are made easier. If we take up this attitude, we shall never be joyful and never experience blessing, for our refusal to rejoice and to praise the Lord now, puts us out of correspondence with the good, and so we are non-receptive to good. What we have to do is to cultivate joy, now; just where we are, and in our present circumstance. As I have already pointed out, in this Psalm, which is a very exalted one, we are not taught to call upon the Lord to bless us, or our soul, but we call upon our soul to bless the Lord. By so doing we vibrate, so to speak, in harmony with the good, the true and beautiful; we become attuned to the Eternal and Real: we become at one with the true Substance, Harmony, Order, Wholeness and Perfection.

We have to find the Divine Key-note in order to enjoy the Divine Harmony. The faithful rendering of a piece of choral music depends upon the singers keeping the right pitch. There is a certain Divine pitch, and there is also a Divine tempo which must be maintained. If we neglect praising and thanking and blessing the Lord we become flat, and tempo becomes slowed down, so that we are in a state of discord.

Most of us have used a gramophone at some time. We know that for each record there is a correct speed at which it must be played. We know also that if we do not wind up the spring, the speed dies down, and then, instead of a correct reproduction of music, we hear a most melancholy and dismal travesty of it. So, also, is it with us, if our soul is not attuned to the highest. It becomes run down, and our whole life suffers in consequence. The Psalmist shows us how we can tune up our soul to the Divine pitch by calling upon it to bless the Lord.

However, it must not be thought that there are no times and occasions when we should pray to the Lord for help and blessing. David, himself, although the writer of the 103rd Psalm, in many other songs, cries unto the Lord and beseeches Him to help him. Such prayers are undoubtedly necessary, especially at those times when we may be in such plights as David often landed himself in. But such prayers are of a lower order than that of the 103rd Psalm. They are good, in that appeal to the Lord, and they are necessary at certain times, especially times of great trouble and distress. At such times, all that we can do is to call upon the Lord to deliver us. But, later on, we may be able to bless and praise the Lord, because He *is* delivering us, and always does deliver us. There are psalms to help us in all our moods, and to supply all our spiritual needs, they have been the sheet-anchor of God's people, down the ages.

With the third verse begins David's recital of all the gracious benefits of God. They are wonderful, even when read in the ordinary way: but they are found to be much more wonderful, when we come to examine them more closely. But this must be left over to the next chapter.

Practise what we know

In the meantime, do not let us be satisfied with just reading about these things, but let us make use of these two verses, daily and hourly: reciting to ourselves:

> Bless the Lord, O my soul,
> and all that is within me,
> bless His holy name.
> And then, when our soul is warmed
> and quickened within us, let us continue:
> Bless the Lord, O my soul,
> and forget not all His benefits.

Through so doing, our soul will become alive, or lively. When this is achieved, we can enjoy God, which is the highest form of joy.

In this chapter I have endeavoured to show how great are the advantages which come to us as a result of blessing the Lord, our true Source and Centre. These advantages, or benefits, as the Psalmist calls them are inevitable. We cannot give anything to God without receiving an hundredfold in return. The more we give the more we receive: it simply cannot be avoided. But, of course, it is hardly necessary for me to point out, that we should not bless the Lord in order to get something in return: but we should do so out of love, and because we want to do so, out of gratitude. "We love Him, because He first loved us". What is termed "cupboard love" defeats its own object, by its own nature. When our object is pure [sincere, disinterested, free from any ulterior motive] then we find God. "Blessed are the pure in heart: for they shall see God".

Finally, let us remember that we must make use of the knowledge that we possess; exercise the powers that we have, and put into practice the Truth which has come to us; for, if we do not, then they pass from us. Divine gifts are given to us only for use. If we fail to use them, we lose them.

CHAPTER NINE

Healing

We have considered together the first 2 verses of the 103rd Psalm. We saw that it is not sufficient for us merely to read the Psalms, and think that they're very lovely, but that we must make use of them - speak them, utter them aloud, address the words to our soul, to wake it up and raise it to a higher plane of consciousness.

It is by the use of words in this way that our vibrations are raised. Everything is vibration - matter, form, light, colour, sound, all are due to vibrations of energy. Everything on this visible plane vibrates at different rates, and in different ways. According to modern physical science, this desk on which I am writing is not the inert mass of dead matter that it appears to be but is a mass of vibrating energy. But this is not all. There are various planes - the physical, the mental, the spiritual, and so on. These vibrate at different rates. Those, therefore, who are of the earth, earthy, vibrate in correspondence to their "earthy" affinities. Those, however, who are spiritually minded can vibrate in harmony with the "spiritual" affinities. By this I do not mean "astral" but Divine. Then there are those who, because they have cultivated Heaven in their heart, are able to vibrate in correspondence with Celestial planes.

The object of the 103rd Psalm is to enable us to make our soul to vibrate in correspondence with God's plane. It bids us exhort our soul to bless the Lord. By so doing our soul is made alive and capable of vibrating in tune with the Celestial vibrations.

Conditions which must be fulfilled

Of course, this state of union with the Divine cannot be brought about if we are not willing to surrender or forsake all those states of mind and heart which separate us from God. We cannot be raised to God's plane if we hate our brother, for instance. This is so because God is love. Therefore, only those who love their neighbour, or fellow man, as well as God, can find God. Man cannot love God, no matter how much he may say or think that he does, if he loves not his brother. "If a man say, I love God, and hateth his brother he is a liar: for he that loveth not his brother whom he hath seen, how can he love God whom he had not seen?" I John, 4, 20.

Neither can we become raised to God's plane, if we cherish anything or desire that is not God-like, such as impurity, self-ishness, covetousness, dishonesty, deceitfulness, love of praise, love of flattery, lust of power over others, love of money, ac-quisitiveness, love of justifying oneself, in addition to even the slightest form of resentment and self-pity. When we have let all these things go and are willing to see ourselves as others see us, and as we appear in the revealing light of Truth, then are we ready to "mount up with wings as eagles".

Of course, we cannot of ourselves, cleanse ourselves of these evil things which drag us down to disease, misery and disintegration; but we can be willing to be cleansed: we can surrender them, we can be willing that the fire of the Spirit should burn away the dross. If this surrender is made, then waiting upon the Lord, blessing His name, and staying our mind upon God, have the effect of transforming us, for we grow into the likeness of the ideal that we worship and adore.

Having released our hold upon all those things which, because they are not of God, and not like God, keep us separate from God, and chain us down to this lower plane, we can become raised up to God's plane of high vibration, through calling upon our soul to bless the Lord.

> Bless the Lord, O my soul,
> And all that is within me,
> Bless His holy name.

Immediately we utter these words our vibrations become raised. We become raised above the lower vibrations of sin, disease and other forms of disorder. Ill-health, sickness, disease, lack, disharmony, ugliness and misery of various kinds, all belong to the lower plane of disorder and disruption which is not of God. The only remedy is to become raised to a higher vibration which is above the realm of disorder, to the realm of order, affection, wholeness and joy. This can be achieved only through love and praise. When we love everybody and everything, and every atom of our environment, then we can love God with our whole heart, and praise Him and be raised above the disorder of life to the order, harmony and beauty of the Divine.

Divine order in manifestation

There was a great manifestation of this in Jesus Christ. His gospel was the gospel of the Kingdom. The Kingdom of Heaven is at hand, is in your midst, is among you, was the burden of His teaching. Love your neighbour as yourself, love God with all your strength, resist not evil, do good to them that hate you, do the will of the Lord of Harmony, and you will find the Kingdom. Everywhere that Jesus went, order and harmony were manifested in the lives of those who were willing to be healed and blessed. These manifestations of beauty, order and harmony, which appeared wherever Jesus went, were manifestations of the Divine order which is the ever-present reality. The same Spirit which raised up Jesus is here present with us to help us find the Kingdom of harmony and order, so that we should all be set free from the powers of disorder. There is no need why we should suffer from any form of disorder. If we follow the teaching of Jesus Christ, then we become set free. To follow His teaching is to find an entrance to a fuller, richer and more abundant, orderly and harmonious life.

In passing, I would like to say that one of the principal causes of man's trouble is that he is always against something or somebody. We have all read of the man who was always against the government, no matter what that government might be. We remember also the boy at school who was always getting into trouble. He was given various punishments, but this did not cure him. He had a terrible time, simply because he was always against all discipline instead of conforming to it or agreeing with it. Consequently, the whole system of school discipline and order was against him. He was in a state of continual boiling rage and resentment, and because of this saw injustice in everything that happened. He could not be brought to see that the cause of the whole trouble was in himself, and that if he had worked in with everybody else, instead of against them, then he would have kept out of trouble the same as all the other boys.

In the same way, many of our troubles are due to the fact that we are against things, instead of in agreement with them. It has been said that man dies because he is not in harmony with his environment. This may be true, or it may not be true, but I am quite sure that many of our troubles are due to the fact that we are against our environment instead of in agreement with it. The reality is harmony, order, unity, love, co-operation, mutual helpfulness. We may think that everything goes wrong or is liable to go wrong with us. This causes worry, care, anxiety, fear, fretfulness, irritability and nervous breakdown. But, actually, the cause of the whole trouble is that we are out of tune with the harmony of life. It is we who cause our own troubles by not keeping in step with life, like the recruit who declared that the whole company was out of step except himself. If we were in love with life, and if we agreed with our adversary, as taught by Jesus, our life would be harmonious and beautiful.

Getting in tune

We can become more in tune with life, and enter into harmony with our environment, by loving and blessing all our fellows, all animals, all creation, in fact. We can spend a few minutes every day in blessing all our environment, and in sending out benedictions of love and compassion to the whole universe. If we practise this, instead of merely reading about it, we not only enter into a harmonious fellowship with the whole, but we also see God everywhere. And, if we are able to see God everywhere it is because God indwells us, for it is with His eyes that we see. In one sense, God can see only Himself reflected, so to speak, in His creation. If, therefore, God indwells us we see God everywhere.

It was because of this that in chapter 1 I suggested that we should call upon all creation to bless the Lord, and also every particle and atom in the universe, and every particle and atom in our body, which is a replica of the universe. By so doing we come into complete harmony with the universe [our environment], and our body, a replica of the universe, also enters into the same state of harmony and wholeness. Because our body is a small replica of the universe, there is a close relationship between them. Therefore, if we are not in harmony and friendly relationship with the universe, it is hardly likely that our body will be whole and healthy. If, however, we are friendly towards life, and in harmony with every atom in the universe, then there is a likelihood of our body expressing the order and wholeness and perfect functioning of the universe.

Practise the truth that we have

The object of the 103rd Psalm other Psalms and hymnodies and canticles is to raise us up to the plane of universal consciousness in which we realise our union with the whole - that is in union with God and all His manifestations. But, of course, we must make use of these things, and not merely read about them.

One of the methods used by the Psalmists was to get the people to praise the Lord and to bless His holy name. This we have in the opening verses of the 103rd Psalm. Another method was to tell of the wonders of Jehovah, what He is, and what He has done. Some of the old hymns have the same object in view, and are almost as robust, positive, strengthening and uplifting as the Psalms. Other hymns for the most part are either theological, or else sentimental, weak, and negative.

The second verse of the 103rd Psalm introduces the second method: *"Forget not all His benefits"*.

It is a call to our soul to remember the marvellous way the Lord has blessed us, what wonderful things He does for us, and how wonderful Jehovah is. By telling of all these things our soul is raised up to that plane where all these wonderful things become possible.

Praise comes first

When we are in trouble, or when we are not well, or when life is difficult, the soul is apt to think in terms of trouble, sickness, and difficulty. Thus, a vicious circle is set up, for such thinking attracts more trouble, more sickness, and more difficulty. The average person says: "I will praise the Lord when I have something to praise Him for". The spiritually wise, however, will praise and bless the Lord and tell of His mighty acts. By so doing he raises his soul to a higher plane, thus making the most wonderful blessings possible. By this I mean, that the blessings are always operating freely and abundantly, but our soul has to become attuned to this state of blessedness or rate of vibration. Or, in other words, the soul has to rise and become capable of breathing the atmosphere that is full of life, health, wholeness, and every form of blessing.

If we are sick, the last thing that we should do is to think, speak and dwell upon our sickness. The remedy is to praise and bless the Lord, until we can feel the vibrations of Divine health and joy. If we are hard up, the last thing that we should do, is to dwell upon our miserable state, or to think in melancholy terms of "hard-upishness". The right thing to do, although it may appear foolishness to the natural mind, is to bless and praise the Lord, and to tell of all His marvellous works, until we feel, in our small way, as opulent as God Himself, who simply expresses all His marvellous manifestations.

The world is mine and the fulness thereof.

The soul gives life and therefore must receive life

Why is this? Because the soul is the source of life to the body; it is also the basis to our life. The body is full of soul, and the soul should be full of God. The soul gives life to the body, and when the soul is withdrawn the body decays. If the soul is not in a state of health, then the body cannot be healthy. If the soul departs from its Lord, then any form of outward disorder or disharmony may manifest.

Therefore, I say that no matter what our trouble may be, it can only be healed by changing the mood of the soul. If the soul is melancholy, then the outward life will be morbid and dark. If the soul is allowed to be depressed, then the outward life will go from bad to worse, always downhill.

The 103rd Psalm gives us the key to the whole situation. If we rejoice in the Lord and bless his name, and "forget not all His benefits", then the soul is healed and brought into a state of harmonious, joyous union with God, and thus becomes filled with the life and health of God.

Who healeth all Thy diseases

There are diseases of the soul as well of "mind, body and es-tate". Such diseases of the soul find expression in the outward life in a variety of forms. The soul can be healed by calling upon it to bless the Lord. Not by reading about it, but by actually doing it.

A time should be set apart every day for the purpose of blessing the Lord and calling upon our soul to bless His holy name. If we persevere with this then in course of time our soul lives in a state of joyous relationship or union with the one Lord of Life, Harmony, and all possible good. God is the supreme good. If, therefore, our soul is in union with God, then good only can come to us, and every cloud has indeed a silver lining, and every experience will reveal the infinite love of God.

Is our soul alive, or are we merely an animated carcass?

We have not yet reached the verse which I thought we should concentrate upon most, and so it must be left over until our next chapter, as it is too great and wonderful to be dealt with in the small space that remains.

Let me close this chapter with this one thought: is our soul a living soul, or are we merely an animated body or carcass? The majority of people that we meet, unfortunately, belong to the latter category. The mind is quite dark, the soul is not yet awakened, and there is not a spark of real life in them that we can be conscious of. The danger is that we, with all our privileges of spiritual revelation, should allow our soul to slumber, so that we join the ranks of the spiritually dead. We know that in spite of the fact that the vast majority of the masses of the people are quite indifferent to religion and spiritual things, yet there is the Hidden Splendour within them, all the time.

When we read of policemen heroically giving their own lives to save the lives of the public, and of relief parties going down into an exploded coal mine in a forlorn hope and a desperate endeavour to save their stricken fellow workers, we worship God, for we see God revealing Himself in the heroism and self-sacrifice. We know that the people are splendid, and that no matter how dead spiritually they may be, yet the Divine Spark is within, and that someday it will be fanned into a flame.

Great watchfulness needed

But, for one who has seen the Lord, and whose soul has been awakened, to allow his soul to fall into, or to remain in a state of stupor and deathly sleep is a tragedy of the first magnitude. Yet, if we do not "watch out" our soul quickly falls back into its sleep of death. Daily, we must do something to counteract the deadly miasmata which infest our path. A time must be spent every day in making use of exercises such as will wake up our soul and keep it awake and vigorous. There is nothing better for the purpose than the 103rd Psalm. Let us, therefore, make use of it, and also other of the Psalms. Our Lord used them, derived strength from them and quoted from them. Also, He spent much time in prayer. If He had not done so He would have failed when He came to the great crisis of His life. How much more necessary is it, in our case, that we also should make contact with the One Father!

Praying for results

But some may say that they want to pray for definite results. They are in great distress and need deliverance. Just so - but the 103rd Psalm is an effective preparation for the kind of prayer that is capable of achieving great results. When the soul is winged upwards to the heights of God and is in perfect harmony and tune with the highest, then we are at the Secret Source of all Power. If the soul is raised in its vibrations until it vibrates with the One Divine Soul of the Universe, then great things become possible.

> And all things, whatsoever ye shall ask in prayer, believing, ye shall receive.
>
> Matt. 21:22

But such asking must be done when we are attuned to the Supreme Good and must be done according to the will of the Supreme Good and must also be done in faith in the Supreme Good, believing that He is able to do exceeding abundantly above all that we ask or think, according to the power that worketh in us. Also, in addition, the prayer must be unselfish, always for a good purpose, for the good of others.

CHAPTER TEN

Renewed Life

C ontinuing our consideration of the first part of the
103rd Psalm we notice the fourth verse:

Who redeemeth Thy life from destruction.

This refers to the soul, of course. The Lord redeemeth the
life of our soul from destruction. "For Thou hast delivered
my soul from death, mine eyes from tears, and my feet from
falling". Psalm 116, 8.

We cannot do it of ourselves: it is only the Lord who can
redeem or deliver. Faith and trust are required of us, but the
redeeming is done by the *Lord*. It was the father who restored
the Prodigal son. The son did not restore himself, but he had
to return to his father, confessing his fault.

It is the Lord, then, who redeems the life of the soul from
destruction. The soul has so many enemies. There are fleshly
lusts. There are spiritual sloth and slumber. There are the
cares and anxieties of life. There is the deceitfulness of riches,
whether we possess any or not. There are also the sins of covetousness, of hate, resentments, of brooding over sorrows, and

so on, for their name is legion. All these antagonistic powers, forces and temptations endeavour to destroy the soul. They are necessary for its growth, unfoldment and development, for no soul can advance, save through the battle of the soul; but they can never overcome the soul if we put our trust in the Lord, and praise His name.

Bless the Lord, O my soul... Who redeemeth Thy life from destruction.

This, of course, should have its influence on the physical life and the physical body, for they are dependent upon the soul, for the soul gives life to the body. If the life of the soul be redeemed, then the body may be redeemed also.

If we are in sorrow, in danger, or in any state of difficulty or distress, the remedy is to bless the Lord, to praise Him and to tell of all His marvellous works. If we are successful in this, and thus able to realise the truth about God, then we are delivered out of our distresses.

Now, let us see how the Psalmist sets about bringing about the desired effect. He begins to state in poetic language, but in short, pithy sentences, the wonderful and glorious things that the Lord does for us. They are a series of surprising and startling statements. Let's examine them, one by one. Here is verse 3:

Who forgiveth all thine iniquities: Who healeth all Thy diseases.

First, we are struck by the fact that these two remarkable statements are bracketed together. They are not promises, but statements of actual ever-present truth. It does not say that if we believe in a certain dogma, or if we perform certain penances, we shall be forgiven and healed. No, it is stated that the process of forgiveness is perpetual and eternal, and that the healing of our diseases is forever taking place. God does not have to be cajoled into forgiving us or healing us - he is continually forgiving and healing, to the uttermost. All that is required of us is that we should realise this glorious truth and accept it.

Continuous forgiveness and healing

Later on in the Psalm the Psalmist amplifies this affirmation of God's forgiveness, by some equally startling statements. He devotes verses 8, 9, 10, 11, 12 and 13 to enlarging upon the loving and complete forgiveness of Jehovah. "The Lord is merciful and gracious ... and plenteous in mercy". "He hath not dealt with us after our sins, etc. "For as the heaven is high above the earth, so great is His mercy toward them that revere Him". "As far as the east is from the west, so far has He removed our transgressions from us". "Like as a father pitieth his children, so the Lord pitieth them that revere Him".

Is it not wonderful? And yet how simple!

The next thing that we notice is that the forgiveness of all our iniquities precedes the healing of all our diseases. Not only does sin cause disease, but also the thought that sin is unforgiven. When the man who was sick of the palsy was let down through the roof, so that our Lord might heal him, the first thing that Jesus said was: "Son, Thy sins be forgiven thee". It was after this that the palsied man was healed of his infirmity, when Jesus said unto him, "Arise, take up Thy bed".

Inward conflict is a cause of disease

The thought of unforgiven sin within the soul, and a sense of separation from God, cause a state of conflict. Inward conflict, although we may be unaware of it, tends to produce disease, or chronic ill health, in much the same way that sin does. We all know that the sin of resentment, brooding over wrongs, bitterness, revengeful feelings, and things of this kind, produce diseases in the body. So also does giving in to the sin of criticism, condemnation, judgement, in fact everything that makes up against life, instead of friendly towards it. But it is not generally known that a realisation of the glorious fact that all our iniquities are forgiven, and transgression removed from us, as far as the east is from the west, is a Divinely appointed gateway to healing. Realising this truth, of instantaneous, ever-operating forgiveness, fills us with joy and peace: we experience a great relief; it removes the cause of inward conflict: and all this makes for health and wholeness, which is the normal or Divinely natural state for us.

Reinstatement

As soon as we confess our sins to the Lord we are delivered from our sins and restored to our original state of sonship. Jesus taught this very clearly in the parable of the Prodigal son. As soon as we return to the Lord and confess our worthlessness, surrendering the false kingdom of self-will which we had built up in opposition to the Kingdom of God, we are accepted, not as a hired servant [someone tacked onto the household but not of it] but as a son. Every possible blessing and favour is heaped upon us.

Becoming Free

Therefore, the Psalmist bids us bless the Lord and call upon all that is within us to bless His holy name because he forgiveth all our iniquities, and healeth all our diseases. Not some of them, but all of them. Every iniquity forgiven, and every iniquity removed from us, and every disease healed. There is no exception, no omission. Bless the name of the Lord.

To the extent that we can enter into a full realisation of this, to that extent do we become free. The 103rd Psalm is designed to help us to that end. Let me repeat, the object of the Psalm is to raise us up to a higher vibration, to a state of joy in the Lord. The more joy we have in the Lord, the more related we become to health, and every other form of good.

O taste and see

But, some may say: "How can I know that my iniquities are forgiven, and my transgressions removed from me, as far as the east is from the west? And how can I say that the Lord healeth all my disease when I am far from well, and my surgeon says that I must go into hospital next week?" The reply to this is that we should put the 103rd Psalm into practice and prove it to be true. If we bless the Lord and call upon our soul to bless His holy name, because He forgiveth all our iniquities and healeth all our diseases, and if we keep on doing so, perseveringly, then we become raised up to a higher plane of joy, in which we find that what we have declared is true. If we do not make use of the means offered us, then we are like a man who with a goblet before him containing the Elixir of Life, refuses to drink, but asks instead: "How do I know that this drink is the Elixir of Life? I don't feel any of its life-giving power; therefore, how am I to know that it contains any?" The obvious answer, of course, is: "drink the contents of the goblet, and then you will know that it contains the Elixir of Life".

Those who want to ask endless questions, or who want to argue about everything, never enter into Truth. The people who want to understand intellectually those things which can never be understood intellectually, but can only be discovered experimentally, obviously can never make any progress.

Heal the soul first

Also, because of its great importance, may I repeat something else? May I repeat that if we want "healing of mind, body and estate", we must change the mood of the soul. I find that if we have some bodily ailment our thought is directed *against* it: or, if we have some trouble, our thought is directed *against* that: or, again, if we have some threat of loss or poverty, that our mind is directed *against* that. This makes matters worse and entails great suffering. What is needed is that we should change the attitude of the soul.

Why should we change the attitude of the soul? Because the outward difficulties and troubles are due to a wrong attitude of soul, or to the soul not drawing its proper nourishment from its Divine Source.

A sick soul means a sick boy. A troubled soul means a troubled life. An impoverished soul means an impoverished life.

Some people look upon this text as applying literally to the physical life. I do not see why they should not do so. The life of the soul is the more important, but, when we are sick or in pain, the health of the physical body seems to be, to us, the all-important thing. After all, our Lord healed all who came to Him for healing. He turned none away. Therefore, it is quite right for us to claim this positive statement, as referring to deliverance from forces which may appear to be destroying our physical life.

For instance, one who reads this may be suffering from a disease which threatens his life. If so, he is quite justified in taking hold of this statement and applying it to himself. "He redeemeth Thy life from destruction".

The object of this Psalm is to bring us into living contact and union with the Lord, by Whom all things were made, and without Whom not anything was made that was made. John 1, 3. The Lord is Life and the Author of life, and is health, wholeness, affection, and also love. The Lord, as love, wants to heal because He is love, and He is *able* to heal because He is Life, Health, Wholeness and perfect order and harmony.

Therefore, whoever may be faced by disease or sickness which threatens his life, is entitled to interpret this verse as applying to his physical body as well as to his soul.

Again, the object of this Psalm is to awaken and increase our faith: it is to bring us to that state of knowing in which we realise that there is an inner and universal Principle and Power, which we call God, and Which is able to answer any prayer, and to accomplish that which is humanly impossible.

All things are possible if we believe them to be possible. Our Lord could not do many mighty works in His own country because the people had no faith in Him. "And he marvelled because of their unbelief". "But", Jesus said, "if Thou canst believe, all things are possible to him that believeth".

Therefore, before anything can become possible, we have to believe it to be possible. We believe that there *is* a Power that can achieve the impossible. The use of this Power has been lost, but the same Power is available - that we firmly believe. Because we believe in it with such fervour, the time will surely come when the use of this Power will be restored, so that the miracle working of early days will become quite the usual thing.

However, to return to our subject. The Psalm says of the Lord: "Who redeemeth Thy life from destruction".

Let us therefore take hold of this statement of Truth, and believe it, and try to realise it. It is one thing to believe it, and quite another thing to realise it. But we must first believe it, and claim it, before we can realise it.

The realisation of the presence of God as Life and Wholeness is a Power that will meet every true need, and every unselfish desire. If our one object is to serve God and to do the will of God, then we are justified in laying hold upon every promise of God, and claiming it for ourselves, and others. We are justified in so doing, for we have no longer any desire to live for self, but only for God, and to bless and serve others.

Life may be challenging many of us at the present time. Some may have come apparently to the end of their tether. If such be the case, then a complete surrender should be made, so that there shall be no desire to live except to serve God and to do His will. A rededication of the life to love and service should be made, and then God's promise may be laid hold of, without any reservation.

He shall call upon me, and I will answer him; I will be with him in trouble; I will deliver him and honour him. With long life will I satisfy him and show him my salvation.

Psalm 91: 15-16.

God never does anything by halves. He not only redeems our life from destruction, but the fourth verse continues:

Who crowneth thee with loving kindness and tender mercies.

How wonderful the Lord is! Not only redeeming or delivering our life from destruction, but also crowning us with His loving kindness and tender mercies. Not merely saving us from destruction; not merely giving us a minimum of what we require; but *crowning* us with loving kindness and tender mercies. The Lord overwhelms us with His goodness.

Thou anointeth my head with oil: my cup runneth over. (Psalm 23, 5.)

Anointed, crowned, how wonderful the Lord is, especially in view of that glorious statement in the Revelation of St. John the Divine, that we are called to be kings and priests unto God!

O, how wonderful is the loving kindness of our God! Who crowneth thee with loving kindness and tender mercies. For as the heaven is high

above the earth, so great is His mercy towards
them that revere Him. (Verse 11)

Immeasurable blessings and inexhaustible love and goodness
are heaped upon us, so that we feel humbled to the dust, when
we think of our unworthiness. But the Lord is ever like that.
When we turn to Him and live according to His laws, and
endeavour to give our little all to Him, we find that blessings
are heaped upon us, to overflowing. Every possible good and
every possible bounty and privilege are showered upon us. We
do not have to run after them, for they push themselves into
our life.

The cause of lack and want in our life is often that we live in a
consciousness of privation. We are so apt to live in a constant
"ache" of longing for better things; by so doing we impress the
sense of privation upon our subconscious mind, thus intensi-
fying it and making it permanent.

The wisdom of the psalmists

The psalmists knew all about this, although they used different
terms to express their thoughts. They knew that this sense of
privation was the cause of privation. They also knew that if
this consciousness of privation were overcome, and replaced
by a consciousness of possession, then bountiful blessings and
all good conditions would come into manifestation.

And this also is why our Lord said: "Therefore I say unto
you, what things soever ye desire, when ye pray, believe that

ye receive them, and ye shall have". By this is meant that if when praying we believe that we have it, then we find that it manifests. This interpretation is confirmed by the Weymouth and Moffat translations, which are as follows: "Whatever you pray for and ask, believe you have got it, and you shall have it". Moffatt. While the Weymouth version reads: "Whatever you pray and make request for, if you believe that you have received it it shall be yours".

The promised land consciousness

What all this means is that what prayer has to accomplish is to change our consciousness from one of lack to one of abundant possession of good. Or, as some would put it, to change from the "Wilderness" consciousness to the "Promised Land" consciousness.

This is the object of the Psalm which we are examining. It is also the object of some other of the Psalms. The Psalmists went about their task in a systematic and scientific way. They knew that if they could only change the consciousness of the masses of the people such a spiritual force for good would be generated that great and wonderful things would happen.

The 103rd Psalm bids us bless the Lord and to call upon all that is within us to bless His holy name. This sets the soul on fire, so to speak, or aflame with love and adoration, and thus it is raised to God's plane, and vibrates in harmony with Divine Good. Following this we are exhorted to recite the greatness and wonders of Jehovah's goodness to us. This goes on until near the end of the Psalm, when the angels are called upon to bless the Lord, and the Heavenly hosts and the ministers of Jehovah, and all the works of the Lord "in all places of His dominion". This final object is to bring the soul into a state of cosmic or universal consciousness, embracing all Nature, the Earth and Heaven.

So, the object of this recital of God's goodness is to raise our consciousness from being one of lack or privation, to a consciousness of possession and abundant good. Therefore, we bless the Lord because He crowns us with loving kindness and tender mercies. By so doing we pass from a consciousness of lack and longing, to one of abundance and Divine Good.

It is not easy for us to do this in the face of great exterior lack and limitation. When the tide of our affairs is at the ebb, and nothing that we can do can stop it, it is not easy to change the consciousness from a sense of lack and fear, misery and apprehension, to a sense of abundant possession, confidence, joy and satisfaction. It is far from easy, I admit, but it is possible. Also, it is the only way of true recovery. If our consciousness becomes changed, then our life becomes Divinely healed and adjusted.

The 103rd Psalm has been given us as an instrument for our use, by the faithful and persevering use of which the difficult change from a sense of privation to one of being filled with the fullness of God can be achieved. Just as it is not possible to play a piano or violin tunefully and correctly without assiduous practise, so also is it impossible to change our consciousness from a sense of privation to one of fullness of God without perseverance and constant use of the means provided for us.

It is useless merely to read about Truth: we can make progress only by putting into practice the Truth that we have, and making use of the means provided.

People write to me sometimes that they have studied this philosophy and that system, and some other cult, but all to no purpose. They infer that the fault is in the philosophy or system; but, of course, the fault is with themselves. My advice to them always is that they know enough in an intellectual way, and that what is needed is not more knowledge of this kind, but that they should put into practice the knowledge which they already possess.

Use the truth that we have

We must always make use of the truth that we have; we must always live up to the Light that we have; we must always go forward to fresh adventures of faith; and we must also practise affirmative prayer, if we are to make progress. The 103rd Psalm is a wonderfully effective prayer and song of affirmation. God has given it to us: let us therefore make use of it, and thus reap the benefits which come to those who really practice truth instead of merely reading or thinking *about* it.

I have used the term "privation" quite a lot in this article. This word, however, is used in a special sense. By it I do not mean a mere lack of the wherewithal to live, but a privation of all good. All that is termed evil is a privation of good. Whatever the form of evil may be, it is simply a lack of God Who is the only Substance and Reality.

There is true Life, Reality and Substance only in that which is good and true. All else is a privation of God. The remedy for all forms of privation is to be filled with God, who is the only Substance, the True Life, and the one Reality.

Scripture has been quoted both in this and other articles to the effect that we are made kings and priests unto God. It has been suggested that that would give people swelled heads and make them act foolishly in consequence. There is no danger of this with any true disciple. The only ones who could get within a thousand miles of such a state of attainment would be those in whom the self had died completely, so that anything of the nature of pride and vain glory would be repulsive in the extreme. One who is a true disciple knows that the higher he is called the more humble he must become; and the greater the service to which he is called, the more completely must he be willing to serve and minister to others. No, there is no danger of such a thing happening, for anyone capable of being puffed up, has not yet started on the real pathway of discipleship.

That is just by the way, however. Now let us pass on to the fifth verse.

Who satisfieth Thy mouth with good things; so that the youth is renewed like the eagles.

Deducting the word put in italics, the first part of the verse reads: "who satisfieth Thy mouth with good". The Psalmist is speaking to his soul. He says: "who satisfieth Thy mouth". By mouth is meant the hunger of the soul, and also the ability of the soul to take in nourishment. Just as the physical body has to feed on the fruits of the earth, in order to live, and to drink, and breathe; so also does the soul, in order to live, have to feed upon God, and to eat the hidden manna and drink the water of life, and breathe the aethers of the breath of God.

And the Lord satisfies our soul with good - the highest and only good. The only real good is God, Who is the Supreme Good. God, therefore, satisfied us with Himself. He gives us His own life. He gives us His own Substance. He changes us so that we become of His own Substance. Regeneration supplants generation.

> As many as received Him, to them gave He power
> to become the sons of God... which were born,
> not of blood, nor of the will of the flesh, nor of
> the will of man, but of God.
>
> St. John 1:12-13

God is the only substance. God is the only life. God is the only reality. Therefore, we have no substance, no life and no reality apart from God. "Life is only in what is good and true". Therefore, as God is the only Good, and the only Truth, there can be no true Life in us except to the extent that we become changed into the Divine Substance. St. Augustine said: "He called men Gods, as being deified by His grace, not as born of His substance". We possess no real life at all, except to the extent that we become changed into the Substance of God [which is the only Substance] through Divine grace. Therefore, we can have no life at all, except through being deified by His grace, for God is the only Life and the only Reality. I use the word Substance in its true and original meaning, signifying that which stands under all appearance, form, and what we call matter. I mean by the term that Reality which stands behind "appearance", and which alone upholds this apparently solid universe.

And the Lord satisfies our soul with Himself, by giving us Himself, and by allowing us to feed upon Him, so that we become of His own Substance, and, because of this become Immortal, because the only True life [God] is in us, and is the only reality about us.

The youth is renewed like the eagles.

This refers to the soul, of course. Because it feeds upon God, and becomes of one substance with God, its youth is renewed perpetually, so that it can never decay, any more than God can decay, because it is of the same substance, and is filled with the only true and real Life, viz., God Who is Life, the only Life and Source of Life.

The youth of our soul is renewed perpetually. This is the literal meaning of the reference to eagles. There was an ancient belief that eagles renewed their youth every ten years. It was believed that they flew high into the sun, and then dived down into the water; and while in the water the old feathers were shed, so that the eagle rose up out of the water with new plumage, and with complete new youthfulness.

It was probably a story or parable told by the priests, the inner meaning of which would be understood only by initiates. It probably referred to the process of regeneration. The eagle flying into the eye of the sun would typify the soul aspiring after God. The plunge into the water would typify the death of the self, and the new birth through the Spirit into a new life.

So we see that there is an esoteric meaning to this ancient belief about the eagles. The life of the soul is renewed by a continual spiritual rebirth. I knew a man once who was very inventive. As a hobby he used to invent and build clocks. One was attached to the electric light mains, and, by making use of a little current, was able constantly to wind itself up. The result was that the clock never required winding by hand, never stopped, and never required attention. In a similar way the life of the soul is continually renewed from God. Fed, nourished, renewed, in and by God, each life is a perpetual youthfulness.

Although this renewal of youth refers to the soul, yet Moses seemed able to make it apply to his body. In the 90th Psalm Moses states that the days of our years are three score years and ten, but he, himself, lived to be one hundred and twenty, and then he did not die of old age or any weakness or infirmity, for his eye was not dim, neither was his natural force abated. From this it would appear that Moses could have lived on indefinite-ly, if it had been necessary for him to have lived longer.

However, our aim should not be to live forever in the flesh, but rather to know God, Whom to know is life eternal. Really, to know God is the end of every quest, the solvent of every problem, the removal of every difficulty, and the healing of every woe. In other words, when we know God, we find that God is the only Reality, and that beside Him there is none other: in other words, there is nothing but God, and God is all there is.

God is Perfect

In the inner understanding, which by the way, generally comes to us as result of passing through great experiences, and through much prayer and wrestling with God, we realise that God is all there is - that is, He is the only Real and True. And so we determine to know God only, for there is none other. It is also given us to realise that God is Good only, and real Goodness, Love, Mercy, Forgiveness, Wholeness, Life, Order, Harmony, every possible beauty and perfection. Therefore, we recognise God only, in His perfection and wholeness, and we refuse to recognise anything else. The imperfection that appears has no Life in it, for true Life is only in that which is good and true. Therefore, because disorder has no Life or Reality in it, we refuse to acknowledge anything other than God in His perfect order and wholeness.

God as Peace

In other words, we realise God as peace, and we enter into God's peace. God can never be anything that is not peace. God is not in anything that is opposed to peace, or which is not of the nature of peace. Peace, however, is not merely absence of disturbance, agitation and conflict but is also perfect well-being, or state of blessedness. In the peace of God everything is in a state of Divine adjustment. "Thou wilt keep him in perfect peace whose mind is stayed on Thee". Our mind is stayed upon God to the extent that we bless the name of the Lord. "Bless the Lord, O my soul, and all that is within me, bless His holy name".

CHAPTER ELEVEN

Affirmative Prayer

When we consider together the subject of Affirmative Prayer, the first thing that we have to do is to define what we mean by such a term. Affirmative Prayer is a statement of truth. It declares, first, that which is true about the Lord, as the Shepherd of souls; and, second, what is equally true about spiritual man who is a child of God. It does not ask for anything; it takes no notice of appearances; it simply states what is eternally true and which cannot be altered.

When I say that we affirm the truth about God, most readers will agree that in declaring that God is love, righteousness, order, perfection, life, power, and so on, and a lot more, we are merely stating that which is true.

When, however, I say that we affirm the truth about man as the child of God, and that he is created in the likeness and image of God, and therefore is just the same as God [although not God], they will not be able to agree, and certainly will not be able to affirm that Man is love, righteousness, order, perfection, and so on. They will have a good reason for refusing to do so, because they will think and say that, obviously, it cannot be true, because man is selfish, sinful, disorderly, imperfect; in fact, the very opposite of what God is.

The truth about spiritual man

Just so. But what we affirm is not the truth about man, but the truth about Man. Not what is true about carnal man, but the truth about Spiritual Man.

Spiritual Man is man as created in God's own image. It is God's idea concerning us, held forever in His Divine Imagination. The outward man of sin and disorder is not the true man, as created by God, but is a product of our own contrary will and false imagination.

Spiritual Man, or God's idea concerning us, held forever in the mind of God, is the reality and truth about us, and is the only thing that is true about us. Therefore, when we declare the truth about Spiritual Man, we declare that which is the hidden reality about each one of us - the Divine Image which we have marred, but which is held in unsullied perfection in the Mind of God.

Because it is Truth alone that is real and permanent it follows that if we declare or affirm the truth about Man, then that which is not true of Man, but which may be true of man [the product of a contrary will and false imagination] tends to disappear. Declaring Truth turns all that is not truth out of the mind, so that it can no longer have any existence.

The object of affirmative prayer is to produce an effect on the mind; to cast out every thought or idea that is not Truth; so that you may know Truth only - that is, to know the only true God and Him only.

Jesus said: "if ye continue in my word then are ye my disciples; and ye shall know the Truth, and the Truth shall make you free". And what were his words? They were: "call no man your Father upon the earth: for One is your Father, which is in Heaven".

The scribes and Pharisees prided themselves that Abraham was their Father. Jesus declared that his followers [i. e., those who had been born of the Spirit] were sons of God.

Affirmative prayer, then, declares what we believe to be the truth about God, as love, wisdom, power, order, wholeness, beauty and perfection, and much more, and also, as that which transcends all these qualities, and anything, no matter how glorious, that we might think about God. Also, it declares what is true about ourselves as beloved children of God, not asserting anything good of ourselves, but, that we are the recipients of good from our Spiritual Father in Heaven.

Look not at appearances, but to God

But this is not all. Affirmative prayer declares what is true about God's Providence and His love and care towards us. By its use we are able to declare what is really true of each one of us, in the face of that which to the senses, appears to be true, but which is the very opposite of what we know to the Divine order. "We look not at appearances, but to the God who controls every circumstance of our life". George Muller used almost exactly the same words, when, according to appearances, he could not proceed because of a thick fog. When the captain of the ship asked him if he did not see how thick the fog was, and how impossible it was for the ship to proceed, George Muller replied that he did not look at the fog, but to the God who controlled every circumstance of his life. As we all know, five minutes after he had prayed for the fog to be cleared, it disappeared, and George Muller was aware of its dispersal without going on deck to see it.

No assertion of self-will

But, some readers will think, perhaps, that the exercise of such power as that might result in things being done, or brought to pass, which were contrary to the will of God. Yes, it certainly might, if self-will, were employed, but the one who prays affirmatively does not assert his self-will, but only states the Truth. He thus allows Truth to manifest in its own way, and not according to human ideas, or the will of the self. Indeed, his sole desire is that the will of God should be done, and not his own will; for the will of God is good-will and can produce only order and perfection; whereas it is his own self-will which has brought his troubles and difficulties to pass.

In all Thy ways acknowledge Him and He shall direct Thy paths.

George Muller refused to acknowledge the fog but recognised only God. He acknowledged that God had made the appointment for him in Halifax, and that if God wanted him to keep it then, fog or no fog, God would enable him to keep it. He refused to acknowledge the fog as being greater than God's purpose; he acknowledged God's supremacy, leaving the working of the miracle to God.

Two kinds of prayer

In the Psalms we find two kinds of prayer - the supplicatory appeal, and the affirmatory statement. Very piteous, at times, are the Psalmist's appeals. Very victorious, at other times, are his affirmations of the love and mercy of Jehovah, and His power and willingness to save.

Both kinds of prayer are helpful. It depends upon the circumstances as to which kind we use. When we're passing through what may be, at the time, a very trying or even terrifying experience, or when stricken and bereaved, all that we can do probably, is to cry, like David, to the Lord, and beseech him for help and succour. But, after a time, if we persevere, we become more composed; and then our faith reasserts itself, so that we can pray more positively and affirmatively. Then, we may even be able to praise the Lord because He has heard us. In the words of Psalm 118, we can say:

I will praise Thee; for Thou hast heard me, and art become my salvation.

Let me say, in passing, that although it is true that George Muller used supplicatory prayer, yet he always adopted the positive attitude, refusing at all times to acknowledge that adverse circumstances could dominate him, or that they had any real power. He acknowledged that all power was vested in God, and that God alone ruled every circumstance of his life. This victorious, faith attitude of George Muller's was in itself a continual prayer of affirmation. As I have stated elsewhere, it was not so much George Muller's prayers, but his attitude of faith that brought to pass the miracles of his life. His prayer was an asking and a receiving: it was his faith attitude that won him the victory.

A difference

But George Muller's supplicatory prayer was not like the beseeching prayer of the Psalmist. David's trouble was often due to his own sin and excesses which landed him into fearful difficulties. George Muller, on the contrary, when once his heart was changed, gave up once and for all his sinful propensities, and never went back to them. Therefore, he did not fall into the anguished state into which David sometimes plunged.

A moment ago, I said that we might find ourselves in a similar state of anguish in which all that we could do would be to call upon the Lord in much the same terms that David employed. If such be the case, then we should pray and not wait. But, while so doing, we should try to reach that higher stage of faith and understanding in which we can state to be true that which we have been praying [supplicating] might be true. David in the 118 Psalm said:

> I called unto the Lord in distress [or out of my distresses]: and He heard me and set me in a large place.

David called on to the Lord and kept on doing so until gradually his fears were overcome, his mind was calmed, and his spiritual understanding opened, so that he entered into Truth [a large place, an expanded consciousness]. After which he was able to say:

> I shall not die, but live, and declare the works of the Lord.

And again, he could say:

> The Lord is my strength and song and is become my salvation.

There is no supplication now, but only the triumphant affirmation of understanding faith.

The object of prayer, of course, is not to persuade God to do anything, although when we are in distress this seems to be the one thing that is necessary. The sole object of prayer is really the bringing of our mind into unison with the Mind of God. When our mind is brought into unison with the Mind of God, Divine order and peace are manifested. If our mind were always in a state of oneness with the Mind of God, then a state of Divine adjustment and Heavenly harmony would be constantly manifested. But, if we could do this, we should be Gods, not men. It is because our mind falls short of Truth that our life manifests disorder. We may reach a state of union when in prayer, but we lose it when we meet the irritations of life. And so we create trouble for ourselves.

Pray without ceasing

The obvious remedy is more prayer and yet more prayer, so that increasingly our mind is made at one with the Mind of God.

When we meet with exasperating or trying experiences we may go all to pieces at first, our mind simply running riot and swirling with thoughts of resentment, or fear, or some other negative emotion. If, however, we get to prayer, and keep on praying, then gradually the mind becomes calmed and disciplined, until at last it is brought into unison with the mind of God, and we can state as a positive fact that: -

The Lord is my Shepherd, I shall not want.

The object of all prayer should therefore be the bringing of the mind into a state of calm, and also into a state of spiritual understanding, so that instead of knowing evil, we know only God, Who is the Supreme Good, and also Perfect Order, Harmony, Beauty, and Infinite Love, Light and Life, and much more.

To know God and God only

This is our principal difficulty - to know God only, for there are so many things which obviously are not God, nor of God, forcing themselves upon our attention, claiming to be reality. A thousand and one things seem far more real to us than God, and yet God is the only Reality. So long as we look upon them as real, and so long as we believe that they can dominate us, so long have they power over us. If we allow them to dominate us, they continue to do so. If, however, we rise above them affirming our unity with the One Reality - the Divine Order and Interior Harmony - then they cease to dominate us. Admittedly, this is not easy, but it is possible. It does not require cleverness, but only persistence and perseverance.

The need for persistence

It requires persistence and perseverance, because there is a tendency for our thoughts, constantly and repeatedly to be dragged down to the level of time, sense and appearance. For instance: if we are the victim of sin, it is not easy to raise the mind from our sin and failure to God and his idea of man which is sinless. If, however, we allow our mind to dwell upon either the sin itself, or our weakness and failure, we are not only cut off from Heavenly Powers, but we attract to ourselves the very evils from which we desire to escape.

On the other hand, if we raise our mind and thoughts to God and His perfect Idea, or Ideal, or Archetypal Man, we are not only open to receive an influx of Divine Life and Power and Love, but also are we cut off from the powers of evil which otherwise would tend to drag us down.

Divine love excluding sin

The Rev. Sheldon Knapp in his many books and pamphlets points out that John Wesley taught a positive gospel of Divine love excluding sin. This doctrine of love excluding sin interests me because it is a positive doctrine. It is positive because it teaches that we can be so filled with Divine love, that we simply cannot sin. Therefore, we are saved from sin and from sinning; and this is a positive achievement. We are filled with Reality, and this excludes sin, which is not an eternal substance, but a privation or lack of the Real and True.

Where love is, there all is present

The affirmative and positive way of dealing with sin and failure, then, is to turn to the Lord and affirm the truth that Divine Love is so filling us that sin is excluded. We ignore the sin and failure, except to repent of them, and confess them to

God. Instead of concentrating upon our sin, we concentrate on the positive fact of Divine Love excluding sin.

Fighting against an evil habit or sin does but make it the stronger. There must be no giving in to sin, of course; but, if, instead of fighting against it, we turn from it and concentrate upon the sinless perfection, affirming that we are so filled with Divine Love that it excludes sin, i.e., makes sin impossible, then, in place of the sin, there grows up its contrary virtue.

This method is positive and constructive. It is positive and constructive, because it fills us with God, the only Reality and Substance, consequently, the cause of sin, a lack of God, a state of privation, is removed by being excluded.

Salvation, the life of God in the soul

If we take an empty jug and fill it with liquid, the emptiness is taken away. It is excluded by the fluid which fills the jug. There can be no emptiness when the jug is filled with substance. It is the same with us, the way to overcome sin, which is a lack of God, a privation, is to become filled with God - to be so full of Divine love that we simply cannot sin - for all sin is selfishness.

Divine life excluding sickness

But it is not sin alone to which this method may be applied. It is equally true as regards healing. The Reality is Wholeness. Disease, sickness, ill health are not things in themselves, they are a privation, a lack of wholeness, a lack of God, Who is

Wholeness Itself. God's life is perfect: it is whole: it is complete. It is impossible for the life of God to be incomplete or lacking in wholeness; or for it to produce anything that is lacking in wholeness, completeness, and therefore health.

We can never find healing by concentrating upon disease. In some quarters it is declared that medical science has not been as successful as it might have been, because it has concentrated too much upon disease, and too little upon health. The more disease is concentrated upon the more complicated it tends to become. On the other hand, the more health is concentrated upon the simpler it is found to be. If health were to engage our first attention, then ways would be found by which people could be made healthy.

The positive way

It is the same with mental and spiritual healing. Health cannot be found by working against disease, any more than we can fill a jug with water by fighting against its emptiness. The only successful way is to invite the Divine life to enter us, and so to fill us, as to exclude ill health, by filling us with God's wholeness.

Sometimes we may be inclined to say: "I have prayed most earnestly about my disease, but I have not been healed". It may be that our prayer has been negative. It may be that we have concentrated upon our ill health instead of upon Divine Wholeness, and, through so doing, may have impressed the idea of disease upon a subconscious mind.

Because of our doing this the disease or ailment may appear to be a great reality - the greatest reality of life. How easy it is for us to fall into the bad habit of speaking of "My heart", or "My Rheumatism", or "My Asthma". Or, again, we may speak of "My Accident" or "My Operation", and so on. Or we may speak of "before my accident", or "since my accident", or "before my operation" or "since my operation". If we do so, then these things become the great event and reality of our life. All our thoughts revolve around them; therefore, they become the pivot of our life. Consequently, our whole life is built on this idea of disease or ill health; and so even our prayers revolve around them also.

But the positive way, such as we find in the 103rd Psalm, for instance, is the very antithesis of all this negative thinking. Instead of a negative dwelling upon disease we are taught to praise the Lord because He heals all our diseases first of the soul, and consequently of the body also, for the soul informs and also gives life to the body.

Bless the Lord O my soul... Who forgiveth all thine in-iquities: who healeth all Thy diseases.

Prayer of an affirmative type, which praises God because he is our healer, our deliverer and our Salvation, changes our mind and alters the character of our thought. God does not have to change, His purposes do not have to be altered, His will, which is always good will, does not have to vary, for "in Him is no variableness neither shadow of turning". God is the unchanging one: it is we who have to become changed into His likeness. It is our mind and thought that have to be conformed to the mind and thought of God.

So, instead of concentrating upon our lack and insufficiency, we praise and bless God because He eternally is our wholeness and sufficiency. All that we need is to be found in Him, Who is the Reality and Substance, the Wholeness and Sufficiency, the life and the health of us all. And so, we praise Him for this. We bless and praise the Lord because He so fills us with His love that our sin is excluded. We bless and praise the Lord because He so fills us with His life and wholeness, that disease and ill health are also excluded. Thus, being filled with God [Reality], that which is not God passes away.

Divine substance, excluding lack and penury

In the same way, lack of the wherewithal to live, and a chronic hard times consciousness can be overcome, not by fighting them, but only by becoming conscious of the Divine Substance as supplying our every need. It only makes matters worse to concentrate upon our lack and penury. It makes matters much better if we concentrate upon the Inexhaustible Substance, endeavouring to realise the Presence of God as Unfailing Substance.

Praise and thanks, not complaints

instead of complaining to God about our lack and limitation we can praise Him for his bounty. By so doing our mind becomes changed, and when our mind becomes changed, so do our circumstances alter. When we realise the presence of God as Substance and Real Supply, then the poverty and privation of our mind are healed, and our life becomes filled with blessing.

> Bless the Lord, O my soul ... Who satisfieth Thy mouth with good things, so that Thy youth is renewed like the eagle's.

By thanking and praising the Lord, rejoicing in Him, and expressing our gratitude to Him for all the blessings of our life, we are brought into relationship with good and abundance, even as our Lord promised. If, however, we complain of our lot, or pity ourselves, or envy those who are more well-to-do than we, or if we concentrate our attention upon our lacks and distresses, then we cut ourselves off from all blessings, so that the privation of our life is increased.

Our Lord gave us the key to the carefree life of unstinted and adequate supply, in His sermon on the mount. He told us that if we would seek first the Kingdom of God and His righteousness, then all things would be added. This means that we have to put God and His divine order first, and find them, and become filled with God. Then, when our life is filled with God, and we realise the Presence of God as the only Substance and Reality, blessing fills our life.

The care-free life

For some inexplicable reason any attempt to accept our Lord's teaching on the subject of Divine supply, as meaning what it says, is looked upon, in some quarters, as heretical. Yet the teaching of Jesus on this matter is as clear as a bell. To the one who asked to be initiated into the carefree life, [eternal life, the inner life in God] our Lord said: "Go and sell that Thou hast and give to the poor, and Thou shalt have treasure in Heaven". If this young man had done this, he would never have lacked any good thing, and in addition would have been delivered from all the cares and anxieties of worldly possessions.

What our Lord wants us to do is to enter into a life that is both abundant [in all the things that are truly worthwhile] and free from care. But we are slow to learn what God wants us to learn, viz., that the one whose life is God-filled need never trouble about supply at all. God sees after the ways and means if we get on with our job in life. It is not our job, neither is it our exertion or cleverness that supplies our needs, but the blessing of the Lord.

Once, George Muller went to visit a poor man who worked early and late to earn a meagre living. This man, although a professed Christian, said that he had to work such long hours, he had no time for prayer or for reading God's word. George Muller told him that it was not his work that supplied his income, but the Lord, and that if he worked less and prayed more, he would be better off.

George Muller had learned the great secret - it is the Lord who supplies our needs, and the more we can realise this, the more carefree does our life become.

Overcoming negative states

Praising God and rejoicing in the Lord raise our vibrations, so that we vibrate more in harmony and correspondence with that Divine state in which there is not, nor has been, nor ever can be, either sin, sickness or lack. Every negative state is due to a lack: it is not a thing in itself, it is a privation, a deficiency of that which truly is. The way to heal such a condition is to praise, thank and bless the Lord for the thing which we apparently lack.

If we lack mastery over sin, then let us just thank God for giving us the victory over all temptation, by filling us with the love which excludes sin. This should be persevered with, even though things may appear to be going from bad to worse.

If we lack mastery over difficult conditions, then let us thank and praise the Lord because He is causing us to come out conquerors and overcomers.

If we lack mastery over ill health, then let us thank and praise the Lord for His Divine Life whose wholeness is expressing itself in our body, filling us with health and inexpressible joy.

If we lack the wherewithal to live and express ourselves in an orderly and harmonious way, then let us praise the Lord, for His bounty, and because He is filling our life with his substance, which is the cause and support of the so-called material substance.

God is the One Reality, the Unfailing, Inexhaustible Source and Origin of all that truly is. Upon Him we can draw for everything that we need. The more we praise the Lord for His blessings, which we apparently need, the more positive our prayer becomes, and the more our consciousness becomes established in Truth.

> Bless the Lord, O my soul,
> and forget not all His benefits.
>
> I thank Thee, Lord, for complete emancipation
> from sin.
> I thank Thee, Lord, for wholeness and health.
> I thank Thee, Lord, for Divine supply of every
> righteous need.
>
> Praise the Lord, O my soul.

Affirmative prayer, praising and rejoicing in God, because every lack is being met and every privation healed, should be continued until there is kindled an inward glow or warmth, and an uplifting joy which carries one out into a liberty and freedom due to release from earthly care.

Our fathers and grandfathers used to term this sense of relief as "knowing that their prayer was answered". It does not matter what we term it, the thing itself is the same, and it is a real experience. When we reach a sense of relief, liberty and freedom through prayer, the spell is broken, and it is only a matter of time for order to manifest in our life.

Affirmative prayer, the same as any other form of prayer, is applicable to every condition and problem. We simply praise and thank God for the thing that we seem to lack, but which we know is ours, and all men's, according to the promises of God.

Ask, and ye shall receive, that your joy may be full.

Ask, and it shall be given you; seek and ye shall find; knock and it shall be opened unto you.

My God shall supply all your need according to His riches in glory by Christ Jesus.

Also by Henry Thomas Hamblin

The Stillness of the Infinite: 18 Meditations to Deepen Spiritual Awareness through the Progressive Reflective Meditation Method

The Secrets of Your Divine Powers: Reconnect with your Spiritual Self to Overcome Obstacles, Heal your Life and Achieve True Success

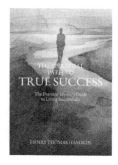

The Spiritual Path to True Success: The Practical Mystic's Guide to Living Successfully

The Message of a Flower: The Divine Wisdom in Nature

The Worry Antidote: The Practical Mystic's Guide to Living Fearlessly

Please visit www.thehamblinvision.org.uk to purchase the following titles:

The Way of the Practical Mystic

The Little Book of Right Thinking

The Power of Thought

My Search for Truth

The Story of my Life

Within You is the Power

Life Without Strain

Divine Adjustment

The Open Door

Life of the Spirit

His Wisdom Guiding

The Hamblin Book of Daily Readings

God Our Centre and Source

God's Sustaining Grace

Printed in Great Britain
by Amazon

57987931R00118